W9-BEA-460

PREPARING TO BUILD

If the ax is dull, and one does not sharpen the edge, then he must use more strength; but wisdom brings success."

Ecclesiastes 10:10

PREPARING TO BUILD

**Practical Tips & Experienced Advice to Prepare
Your Church for a Building Program**

Stephen Anderson

3rd Edition

ISBN: 978-0-9839204-0-3

Library of Congress Control Number: 2011914802

Copyright © 2006, 2007, 2011 by Stephen Anderson. All rights reserved.

No part of this publication may be reproduced, distributed or published in any form or by any means, electronic, mechanical, photocopying, recording, scanning, or otherwise, except as permitted under Section 107 or 108 of the 1976 United States Copyright Act, without the prior written consent of the author.

Published in Clayton, NC, United States of America by Anderson Marketing, Inc. Requests for information or reprint permission should be directed to the author by email at steve@preparingtobuild.com

Limitation of Liability/Disclaimer of Warranty: While the author has used his best efforts in preparing this book from sources believed to be accurate and reliable, there is no representation as to the accuracy, adequacy, or completeness of this information. The advice and strategies contained herein may not be suitable to your situation. Neither author nor publisher is responsible for any errors, omissions, or results obtained from the information contained herein, and disclaim any implied warranties of merchantability or fitness for use for a particular purpose.

Cover design by:
Catalyst Marketing Communications - www.catalystad.com

Architectural artwork used by permission of:
Church Development Services, LLC - www.churchdevelopment.com

Dedicated to helping churches

in advancing the Kingdom of God

and winning Souls for His Glory

With Special Thanks

To my best friend and dear wife, Candace, who encourages me in so many ways, not the least of which was in the writing of this book.

To my dear Mom and Dad, without whose love and sacrifice none of this would be possible.

To my Lord and Savior for the calling and His equipping in my life, for truly *"Faithful is He that calleth you, who also will do it."* 1 Thessalonians 5:24

Table of Contents

Foreword

In church ministry, the phrase "Building Project" can raise emotions of both excitement and dread. The excitement comes because a building project has the potential to grow a congregation's faith in God like nothing else can. They tend to dream about the ministry potential of the new space and what God is uniquely calling them to do for His kingdom. The congregation will often pray, sacrifice, and invest in the life and ministry of the church in such a way that the on-looking community can't help but notice. Yes, building projects are exciting.

While exciting, building projects can also evoke some serious emotional dread. They have the potential to be poorly led, put excessive financial strain on a congregation, and severely damage relationships. Too often we hear the horror stories of churches that split and projects that never get completed. Building projects also can strain the pastoral staff! One statistic thrown at me when we were starting our program was that 83% of pastors leave their church within 12 months after the building project is completed, either because of personal burnout or the relational damage during the project. Maybe dread isn't a strong enough word...

Factually, pastors and their leadership teams often lack the "nuts and bolts" know-how of building programs. The concepts of budgeting for construction, reading architectural plans, leading capital campaigns, and working with contractors are foreign to many church leaders. This leaves us wide open to poor decisions which could cost a congregation thousands of dollars in unnecessary costs, months of extra work, and compromised relational trust.

That is why both Stephen Anderson and his book, *Preparing to Build*, are such a blessing to the Church. From personal experience, Stephen's insight and principles helped us realize the purpose God had in our building project. Stephen first laid out the realities of a building project, and then gave us practical and orderly steps to take. He showed our church leadership teams how to lead in such a way our people felt a strong sense of ownership in the project. He stressed cultural sensitivity and gave us latitude to make the process personal. Ultimately, he helped us discover the answer to the all important question, "What is God calling us to build for the sake of vision fulfillment in the context of what we can afford?" And he did this while never letting us forget what we are about is truly is "Bigger than a Building!"

Like Jethro being a blessing to Moses, Stephen's insight, experience and principles will be a blessing to so many pastors and church leaders who believe God is leading them to trust Him in a building project. Before entering into your building project, as a leadership team I urge you to prayerfully read and apply *Preparing to Build* to your unique ministry context. It will be the best first step you can take if God calls you to believe in him in for a building journey that lay ahead.

Dr. Paul W. Smith
Lead Pastor - Warner Alliance Church, Lewiston, ID

Preface

The Call

I am often reminded of a short encouragement that Paul wrote to the church 1 Thessalonians 5:24, *"Faithful is he that calleth you, who also will do it."* I know that I know God has called me to minister to His church in His name for His glory. He has both called and equipped me for the work of helping churches expand their ability to reach the lost and disciple the saints. The calling is His, the equipping is His, and the Glory is all His.

As a result of having spoken with literally thousands of people over the years about church building programs, God has provided me both insight into the process and an appreciation for how desperately many churches need wise counsel regarding building. I am privileged to be used in this process, but the glory belongs to Him

The secret to a successful building program is to be found in the planning and preparation process; you must plan well in order to build well. Unfortunately, many church leaders are neither equipped by training or experience to lead their church to the optimal conclusion of a building program. This is further complicated by the fact that *churches don't even know what they don't know.* Ignorance is bliss and many churches blissfully enter into building programs only to be rudely educated later in the process. My motivation for writing this guide is summed up in these three statements...

- Building is not easy and mistakes can be very costly to the church emotionally, spiritually, and financially.

- Very few churches have the knowledge, training, or sufficient experience to minimize the cost, risk, and effort of building.

- I desire to minister to your church to help it become the vision and accomplish the mission God has planned.

In the mid 90's I approached my pastor and shared my thoughts about how our small but growing church needed to make plans for getting out of the rented school in order to expand our ministry. We needed to prepare for growth, and even more importantly, not be dependent on the grace of the school district to have a place in which to hold church.

My proposition was we needed to plan for the future, become financially prepared to build, find some land, and build a building where we could "do church" seven days a week instead of 3 hours on Sunday. He wholeheartedly concurred, and to demonstrate that no good deed goes unpunished, he placed me in charge of the building team.

At that time I knew next to nothing about building a church, and thankfully I recognized that important fact. My lack of knowledge drove me to begin the process of discovery, learning, and experience gathering that continues even to this day. Looking back, it is easy to see the hand of God on my life preparing me for not only that responsibility, but also for the calling He put on my life to minister to churches in their building programs.

In my research, one of the things the Lord did was lead me to a small Christian firm dedicated to helping churches build. I was very impressed with what they did for our church and God began to call me to the same work. After much prayer and wise council, I quit my corporate job at the pinnacle of my career to work with them for a season. As that organization eventually changed focus and direction, I was led to start my own firm to continue what which I felt called to do, ministering to other churches in their building programs in God's name for His glory. Through this book, I would like to share some of what I have learned:

- Leading my church through this process.
- Talking to other churches about their building programs.
- Working with like-minded professionals.
- As a consultant/coach working on church projects both large and small.

One of the many things that have been impressed upon me over and over again is how consistently churches end up making the same types of mistakes. I have found most of these mistakes are the product of a poor process caused by a lack of practical experience. Fortunately, this is a problem that is readily solved if the church will seek qualified assistance.

I need to be clear that this book is only a high-level guide; it is not a comprehensive "how-to" manual on church construction, which would take an encyclopedia set, not a book. What this is, however, is a book that will minister to churches with a need to build and help prepare them for that task. I believe God called me out of the world to minister to His church and help equip it for its mission of winning souls for the Kingdom of God. Along with my church consulting services, this book is one of the ways for me to accomplish that task.

One of the things you may notice throughout this book is the number of times I strongly encourage the church to get some expert help. This is neither meant to be self-serving nor undue criticism of the church, its leadership, or building committee. Church leaders often need help because they are taught exegesis of the Word and pastoral care, they learn how to marry and bury, and they get instruction on church planting and church growth strategies; however, no one teaches them what to do when they are successful and need to build! It is my hope that this guide will, at least in part, help meet that need.

As a leader in your church, if you were to perform an impartial assessment you would probably determine that, as a whole, the church leadership team does not have the *real world practical experience or training* to know the proper questions to ask, how to translate those answers into an effective building plan, and then execute that plan in the most effective manner. Simply but directly put, most church building committees lack the "across the board" combination of church growth, financial analysis, church design, and church construction experience to effectively and objectively guide a building program to its best and most successful conclusion.

There is a tremendous need for this type of help - whether the church realizes it ahead of time or not. If you had seen what I have seen and heard the things I have heard over the years about churches getting in financial trouble, getting ripped-off by people who knew more about building than the church, disheartened congregations, wasted time, and effort, and churches split down the middle, then I believe you would have the same burden to help as I have.

Special Building Challenges for Today's Church

The majority of churches planning on building today will find themselves in the position where they need to do *all of the following* without the benefit of either substantial training or experience:

§ Determine all of the proper steps that need to be taken in a building program, *and then…*

§ Learn how to accomplish those steps in the proper order, *and then…*

§ Execute those tasks with excellence *the first time*!

In its totality, this is a daunting set of tasks; and unfortunately ones the church rarely executes as well as it should. Due to a lack of experience, churches often start down a bad path without even being aware of it. From my experience with other churches I can confidently state that it is usually very painful and expensive for churches to backtrack and recover from a poor beginning. It can be terribly embarrassing and painful to stand in front of a congregation and inform them that the building plans presented to them cannot be built.

This is not a hypothetical problem: *Millions of dollars every year are wasted on architectural plans that are never built by the churches that paid for them.*

Those who have worked with me in the past have heard me tell churches over and over again that getting answers to questions is easy; it is knowing what questions to ask that is hard!

You are probably reading this book today because you are...

- Thinking of building in the future and you are looking for good information in order to better understand the process.

- Ready to begin a building program and are looking to discover the "what" and "how" of building a church.

- Already in a building program and beginning to realize the water you jumped into is cold and deep, and you are looking for help.

- A denominational resource looking for building tips or insights to assist in your work with your member churches.

Regardless of the reason you are reading this book, I believe it will be of great help to the church. Regretfully, the further the church is already into its building program, the less helpful this information may be in *this* building program. The reason for this is quite simple; the majority of this book is about what to do before you start the design and construction of your new church, as this is when the most basic and fundamental assumptions and decisions are made and when ideas can be implemented at the lowest cost.

Any builder will tell you that a good building can't be built on a bad foundation. Likewise, projects that do not start off well tend not to end the well. The goal of this book is to get the church started on the right path and outline a process to help the church understand where it needs to go and how to get there, providing that firm foundation on which to build.

The Wisdom of Solomon

If the church does not have substantial experience at building, where should it turn? Whether it turns to a denominational resource or independent consultant, *the church often needs to look outside the walls of the church for wise counsel.* Remember, very few churches have the "across the board" experience in needs analysis, finance, design, and construction in order to adequately minimize the cost and effort of a building program.

Through wisdom is a house built; and by understanding it is established… For by wise counsel thou shall make thy war: and in multitude of counselors there is safety. (Proverbs 24:3, 6) Once you go through a building program, you may have a much better appreciation for the war reference. A question for discussion is how your church will work out this Proverb in its building program.

As we look at the examples of two famous men of God in their building programs, we learn something of importance; both Moses and Solomon got outside counsel and assistance in their building programs! In Exodus 31:1 we see that God provided Moses with an expert to lead his project with *"the Spirit of God, in wisdom, in understanding, in knowledge, and in all manner of workmanship."*

Later, Solomon, in his wisdom, recognized the need for someone experienced to help him with his building program. When he proposed to build the temple after the death of King David, the first thing he asked of the King of Tyre was for help from someone with the type of skill that only comes from experience:

"But who is able to build Him a temple, since heaven and the heaven of heavens cannot contain Him? Who am I then, that I should build Him a temple, except to burn sacrifice before Him? <u>Therefore send me at once a man skillful</u> to work in gold and silver, in bronze and iron, in purple and crimson and blue, who has skill to engrave with the skillful men who are with me in Judah and Jerusalem, whom David my father provided." (2 Chronicles 2:6-7)

With respect to building, there is one particularly noteworthy difference between these two great men of God. As portrayed in the 31st chapter of Exodus, it does not seem to occur to Moses to ask for help. It seems that God had to "volunteer" someone for him; He had to tell Moses He was sending him help in the form of Bezalel. On the other hand, Solomon was wise enough to know *even extraordinary wisdom was no substitute for experience*, so he sought a skilled man to help direct his building program, and God provided Huram.

In the latter part of the very next verse, I believe Solomon provides a good example of the church working with outside experts where he says, *"Also send me cedar and cypress and algum logs from Lebanon, for I know that your servants have skill to cut timber in Lebanon; and indeed my servants will be with your servants."* (Chronicles 2:8) I believe that what is described here was the church bringing in the experienced help they needed which labored *along side* of the church to maximize its results.

As you enter the realm of church construction, you may find that the water is deeper and colder than it looks. My hope is this book will impart some wisdom and understanding to your church, help you ask the right questions at the right time, and possibly, to seek your own Bezalel or Huram to lead your church through a building program with minimal effort and maximum results.

Skill, birthed out of experience, is a precious commodity. Keep in mind the Wisdom of Solomon and give serious consideration to seeking experienced help for your building program. Outside resources will have the real-world experience, the tools, and proven process that will help *objectively* determine the best solution for your church. Prayerfully consider how God provided experienced help to both Moses and Solomon in their building programs and how He can do the same for you.

Beginning with the next chapter is an explanation of a proper process that will help prepare your church to build. We will then continue on to discuss vision, mission, needs, and wants. We will provide an introduction to the process of how to determine if you should build, what you should build, what you can afford to build, and how to pay for it. You will be provided with general church building guidelines which, while generic in nature, will give you a general idea of space and land requirements. Speaking of land, we will discuss land purchase options as well as some special considerations for smaller churches that may be looking at building their first church.

Now please fasten your seat belt and return your seat and tray to their full upright and locked position - we are about to take off!

Chapter 1 - What is *Prepared to Build?*

What Does It Mean to Be Prepared to Build?

Being prepared to build, in its simplest terms, means the church has objectively quantified as many of the variables as possible and developed a building strategy within the financial ability of the church.

A church that is prepared to build will have graduated from *I think* to *I know*. A church that is prepared to build:

§ Can articulate, based on factual analysis, what it needs to build to meet future needs.

§ Understands the cost of construction.

§ Has measured its financial ability.

§ Knows the vision can be built on the selected property.

As you read this book, you will often notice the not infrequent use of the adjective, *objective*. When making decisions that total hundreds of thousands or millions of dollars, you need to avoid making them based on feelings or opinion. The fruit of an objective process is in *knowing* what you need to build and why, what you can afford to build and how you will pay for it, where you will build, and when you will build.

The result of an objective process is objective fact. In the absence of an objective process, all a church is left with is subjective opinion, and in a church of a few hundred people you will have lots of opinions. In the absence of objective fact, any person's subjective opinion is just as valid as another, which makes it difficult to develop consensus.

An objective and fact based process will chart a clear and unequivocal course and provide clear criteria against which you may evaluate options and make decisions.

Proper Process Prevents Poor Performance

An already difficult task can become quite painful by not understanding or adhering to a good process. It does not matter whether you are baking bread, building a space ship, or trying to build a church, *you get better with experience because you discover and apply the <u>best practices</u> that make the job easier and your effort more effective.* This is why experience is such a valuable commodity.

If your church follows a proper process of doing first things first, your building experience will be a much more positive and rewarding one. When most churches think about building, they first call an architect or builder and jump feet first into building design. Doing this puts the proverbial cart before the horse, often leading a church down the path of developing a building plan it cannot afford or does not truly meet the needs of the ministry. ***Until the church objectively understands its real space needs within the context of financial ability, it has no objective way to evaluate any building design.***

I was surprised to learn how many pastors, when they take their new position in a church, find one or more sets of building plans that were never built. A church builder once told me that in his break out session at a church building conference, 20 out of 22 pastors raised their hands when asked if there were un-built plans sitting in a drawer or closet when they took over the pastorate. It is heartbreaking to see the bad fruit that churches reap from a bad process.

The fruit of a poor process can be bitter indeed. I cannot begin to recount the number of churches I have visited or talked with over the years that have each spent thousands or tens of thousands of dollars on plans that will never be built. In two specific instances I know of, a church and a seminary each spent over $100,000 on architectural and engineering services only to find they could not come anywhere near being able to afford the project as designed. Millions of church dollars are wasted every year on plans that will never be built! Don't become just another statistic! Look before you leap, or in this case, plan before you build.

Many times churches get to the point of realizing they can't build and blame the lender, architect, or builder, when in fact the root fault is the church and its implementation of a poor process and poor planning.

God is Not the Author of Confusion

If things don't seem to be coming together for your church in its building program, it is quite likely that you have gotten some things out of order or missed an important step in the process.

One could successfully argue that most of the problems experienced by churches in building programs have their roots in poor planning and preparation. Poor preparation can foster a lack of unity and confidence, ruin pastors, increase building costs, and in general, make an already difficult task much harder.

Poor preparation will result in more confusion, wasted time, increased stress and effort, and at worst, can cause a church split. The key to proper planning is to first correctly understand your needs, abilities, and limitations. There are five basic steps to a church building program and if you get them out of order, things get a lot harder.

Step 1 – Planning: Plan well in order to build well! Understand what you need, what you want, what you can afford, and what your land will support. This prepares you for the next steps.

Step 2 – Fundraising: Few churches are adequately prepared financially to build and/or to retire debt. Until you objectively define the space and financial need, you are not prepared to ask your congregation to financially support a building program.

Step 3 – Design: Until you can define need, financial ability, and what your land will support, designing a building is a waste of time and effort. Generally speaking, design is not the first step, as many would seem to believe.

Step 4 – Finance: To get a construction loan you will first need building plans from which you can obtain an estimate of cost to build. To do that, you need plans that are relatively complete. Few lenders will want to loan money to a church body that is not financially behind the program and many require a capital campaign to be in place for the church to qualify for a loan.

Step 5 – Construction: When *all* the other pieces are in place, then you can finalize your construction plans and begin construction.

The Key to a Better Building Program

The key to a successful building program is found in proper planning. Performing a needs and feasibility study is one of the first steps towards creating a more satisfactory outcome. Quoting from the 2006 FIRST study done by the Rainer Group:

> *"We did find a strong correlation in overall satisfaction with the building project if a feasibility study was conducted. The disappointment, however, is that only one-third of the churches conducted a feasibility study."*

When a consultant says there is a strong correlation, the implication is generally one of cause and effect. In this quote, the operative phrase is *"if a feasibility study was conducted."* This squarely identifies a causal relationship between proper preparation and maximized satisfaction. They were satisfied <u>because</u> they conducted a feasibility study.

According to the study, 33 percent of the churches conducted feasibility studies. This correlates closely to the 35 percent that considered the building process as "excellent" and the 40 percent that indicated the building program created no conflict in the church. I don't believe it is a coincidence that those who planned better were happier with the outcome and had less conflict when building, do you?

Proper planning brings unity to the church and provides the foundation for the design and construction process. In proper planning is found the key to maximizing the church's satisfaction while minimizing risk.

Poor planning will often be found at the heart of cost overruns and financial duress. Failure to properly research and objectively understand the needs of the church and its financial ability can cause the church to build facilities that are too small, too large, or otherwise inadequate. Failure to take adequate preparation in hiring the architect or builder can yoke the church to a poor performer or an improper relational fit. Failure to ask the right questions during the planning process will cost the church time, effort, and money - or worse.

The cost to implement changes in the project increases dramatically as the project timeline progresses. The further the church has proceeded down the path of design and construction, the more expensive revisions become. In fact, one of the major causes of cost overruns in church construction is change orders once construction has begun. It is far easier and cheaper to plan the project correctly in the earliest phase than to implement changes further into the design or construction process.

The following two diagrams clearly demonstrate that the time when the church will have the most impact on the project plan at the lowest cost is early in the planning and design process. *Unfortunately, this is the time when the majority of churches often neglect to get professional assistance!* This can result in changes and corrections getting pushed into the more expensive phases of the project, thereby raising the total cost of the project.

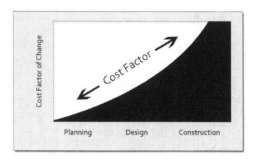

The further along the church is in the building program the higher the cost of implementing change.

● ● ●

Meanwhile, the cost-effectiveness of the church's ability to affect changes in the outcome of the building program quickly decreases.

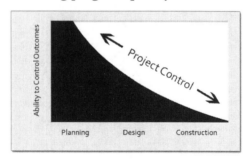

Failure to Plan = Planning to Fail: The fruits of poor planning are:

§ Lack of unity and/or confidence

§ Damage to pastors and other leaders

§ Increased cost

§ Increased effort

§ Increased risk

§ Increased stress

§ Increased conflict

§ Financial problems

§ Facilities that do not meet the needs of the ministry

§ Reduced satisfaction with the completed project

Before you start, you need to know how you will finish. In Luke 14, Jesus gives us the example of counting the cost of building so we do not fail and be thought a fool (and be a bad witness). *"For which one of you, when he wants to build a tower, does not first sit down and calculate the cost to see if he has enough to complete it? Otherwise, when he has laid a foundation and is not able to finish, all who observe it begin to ridicule him, saying, 'This man began to build and was not able to finish.'"* (Luke 14:28-30)

We are going to revisit this biblical example later in Chapter 6 of this book as we discuss financing, but right now it is important to remember that counting the cost for a building program involves organizing and planning.

John Gill, the famous Bible expositor, had this to say about this particular passage of scripture, "Now what person acting deliberately in such a case as this, and proceeding with intention and design, *sitteth not down first, and counteth the cost, whether he have sufficient to finish it;* as every wise man would, who has any thoughts of building a tower, or any other edifice."

However, before you can count the cost, you need to know what you need to build. Building a church today is much more complicated than it used to be. Your church certainly cannot "wing it" with a project budget of six, seven, or possibly eight figures! Sketching a floor plan on a napkin and looking for land seems so easy, and it can be; however, that's a *very* long way from being prepared to execute a building program in an effective manner.

As you will discover when you build, the foundation must be laid before everything else is built upon it. Just so, there is foundational preparation at the beginning of the process of planning to build.

> There is an order of precedence in building that determines what should be done, and in what order, so that the building program is executed in an orderly, objective, and cost-effective fashion, having being built on a firm foundation.

Proverbs 24:27 has this to say about doing first things first: *"Prepare your outside work, make it fit for yourself in the field; and afterward build your house."* Your church should consider the application of this proverb to the building program and be reminded there are preparatory steps that must be taken in order to build on a firm foundation. While some of these steps overlap, the general process is one of:

1. Research & Planning
2. Conceptual Design
3. Fundraising
4. Final Design
5. Financing
6. Construction

The above list is not meant to be all-inclusive, nor is it necessarily chronological or distinctly sequential. Some churches will have to look for land and some will have to sell their current locations, while others have to consider their Christian schools, denominational restrictions, or other outside factors. There are certainly times when more than one of these steps will happen somewhat concurrently. Each church has different needs and starts from a different point. *There is no one-size fits all solution*, that's why experience plays such a huge role in building.

If this "order of service" is followed, the church should expect to:

§ Avoid costly mistakes.

§ Build unity in the leadership and body of the church.

§ Increase financial support.

§ Minimize stress, uncertainty, and confusion.

§ Enjoy the fruit of a good process: a happy and more unified congregation, and a building that best meets the needs of the ministry and its budget.

It's one thing to know the basic steps - it's another to do them well. Your church knows it needs to design a building, but it doesn't really know how to do so. The church knows it needs to hire an architect, but it doesn't necessarily know how to hire the right architect. The church knows it needs to build, but not how to build effectively.

Important concept: The *gap* between knowing and not knowing what to do is much smaller than the *gulf* that lies between knowing what to do and knowing how to do it.

An analogy I often use is that of two airplane pilots. One pilot can quote technical manuals forward and backwards and has spent time in a simulator. The other is an instructor with thousands of hours of actual flying experience. *Who would you want flying your plane?* The same concept regarding experience should apply to your church and who pilots its building program.

In the opening pages of this book I quote Solomon from Ecclesiastes 10:10, *"If the ax is dull, and one does not sharpen the edge, then he must use more strength; but wisdom brings success."* The application of wisdom "sharpens the ax" to make the process easier. Today, we would probably say "work smarter, not harder." Abe Lincoln understood this principle very well and is quoted as saying, *"Give me six hours to chop down a tree, and I will spend the first four hours sharpening the axe."*

The Preparing to Build Process

The fundamental pre-construction process can be summarized in the following points:

§ Understanding how the vision for the church dictates a need to build.

§ Understanding what the church can afford to build and how the church will pay for it.

§ Understanding what the church needs to build and why the proposed solution is the right thing to build to meet the needs of the ministry.

§ Developing a building design driven by the church's needs, but within the framework of what the church can demonstrably afford.

§ Starting a capital campaign.

§ Securing a financing commitment.

Then, and only then, are you _really_ prepared to build, having followed a process that provides the firm foundation on which to do so.

Chapter 2 - Avoiding Common Mistakes

From concept to completion, your church will not undertake a more demanding or complicated task in terms of money, risk, and effort than it will in a building program. The proof of this is often found in the number of pastors who leave churches during or shortly after a building program.

Building a church is a commercial development. You have all the challenges and regulations to meet, just as if you were building a movie theater or Wal-Mart. Your building program must be approached with prayer, planning, and wise counsel, and it needs to be run in a way that will maximize effectiveness while protecting the pastor and other leadership. Your building program needs to be run correctly from the beginning and done right the *first* time, as mistakes and do-over's in construction are prohibitively expensive.

There's Nothing New Under the Sun

Speaking with hundreds of churches about building programs allows one to understand in a unique way the wisdom in Ecclesiastes when the author says, *"There is nothing new under the sun."* While each church's challenges may seem unique to its church members, the reality is that most churches face variations of the same challenges. Many of them also make the same general types of mistakes simply because they don't know any better.

While church building projects cost hundreds of thousands or millions of dollars, mistakes don't just have serious *financial* consequences. Mistakes in a building program can be very costly, not just in terms of money, but also in the functionality of the finished facility, loss of confidence in leadership, and increased conflict or disunity in the body of Christ. A large portion of mistakes made by churches today can be summarized into a single category – the failure to properly plan. Poor planning creates a faulty foundation on which to build.

Quite often the church will create a vision committee or long-range planning committee and task it to present a plan to the congregation. Regretfully, even the best intentioned of committees generally do not have the training or experience to plan and execute a building program in a manner that *best* meets the needs and financial ability of the church. This is nothing against the volunteers on the committees; it's just unfair to expect these people to have the unique skills and know-how that can only come from experience.

Common Mistakes in Church Construction

The common mistakes made by churches fall into 5 basic categories. We will look at each in turn and in the general order that the church will typically make them.

Mistakes of Perception:

The first category of mistake is best described as *perceptual*. The church fails to perceive the complexity of the project for what it really is. The old saying is true, "Ignorance *is* bliss." The church just does not know what it does not know. Sadly, ignorance is bliss only in the very early stages of the project. As the project progresses and the church must deal with a seemingly never ending series of unforeseen issues, bliss can quickly turn to painful reality.

There are five statements regarding perception that are more or less truisms which are applicable to every church building program.

1. Start to finish, the process will take longer than you think it should.

2. The process of building is harder and more complex than you realize.

3. The design and construction of your facilities will cost more than you think it should.

4. Drawing building plans is <u>not</u> the first step in the building process.

5. Borrowing money is much more difficult than you thought.

Mistakes in Planning:

The second category of mistake would be best summarized as *planning* mistakes. Planning mistakes range from making decisions based largely on subjective feelings instead of objective process, to failing to understand what the church can truly afford to build.

In the absence of an objective process, the only criteria a church has for making decisions is subjective opinion. Basing a million dollar building program on opinion is unwise at best and devastating all too often.

Churches that spend months and years *talking* about building instead of *actually* building usually do so because they lack an objective way to determine what should be done. After all, how can one know they hit the target if they don't even know what the target is?

Design Mistakes:

The third of our five categories of mistakes would be *design* mistakes. Design mistakes are the natural outcome of poor perceptions and/or poor planning. The most common design mistake is to enter into the design process before objectively understanding need and financial ability.

The vast majority of the churches that begin the design process without objectively understanding needs and financial ability will end up with a set of church building plans they cannot afford to build. Each year, many millions of dollars are wasted by churches on building plans they cannot afford to build because they engaged in design before they engaged in proper planning.

Financial Mistakes:

One good thing about the economic collapse that began in 2008 is churches have a harder time making serious *financial* mistakes with respect to church financing. Church lenders are fewer and farther between than any time in recent memory and the lending criteria has become so arduous that churches will have a much harder time getting in over their heads financially.

Many of you will read this and say to yourself you are fortunate to have a good relationship with your bank. While you may indeed have a good relationship with someone at your bank, you are far less likely to have a good relationship with the person who potentially approves your loan request. Even if you do have a good relationship with the loan underwriter, I can guarantee you do not have a good relationship with the banking regulator or inspector who is breathing down *that* person's neck.

Two major financial mistakes church often make are not understanding what you can afford to build, and its close cousin, not understanding realistic construction costs. It never ceases to amaze me how large a disconnect we observe between the church's financial perceptions, and the realities of what construction costs are and what the church can afford. If I had a dollar for every church of 50-100 people that wanted to build a building that would cost a million or more dollars I could make a nice down payment on a church! It is amazing the number of people who would never dream of trying to build a million dollar home on a $100,000 income that don't think twice about trying to build a million dollar House of God on tithes and offerings of $100,000!

Construction Mistakes:

Our final category of mistakes is that of construction. Construction is the end of the line, the last step in the process. *Being the last step in the process, this is where many of the other mistakes will come home to roost.*

Just as a snowball can become an avalanche, so a mistake in planning can grow to become an expensive issue in the building process. On top of the snowball effect, mistakes in contracting methods will often cost the church tens or even hundreds of thousands of dollars. We will discuss contracting in Chapter 8 which deals with construction.

Important Concept: A wise person learns from their mistakes, but a really wise person learns from the mistakes of *others*. As pointed out earlier in the discussion on Solomon, experience is more valuable than wisdom alone. Sometimes the first step in wisdom is recognizing what you don't know. Just as Solomon, and Moses before him, received wise and experienced counsel for their building program, so should your church.

Chapter 3 - Forming a Building Committee

Long before actual construction begins, possibly even before the congregation at large is overtly aware of a building program in the works, the church must form a building committee. This is an important task; a building committee that is either poorly staffed or ill-equipped can delay or sidetrack a building project, cost the church money, or even end up splitting a church (no pressure, right?). In this chapter we will discuss various ways to form a building committee and how to staff it with the right people.

Whether you call it a building committee, expansion and relocation team, vision committee, or any number of other names, the church needs to put some good people in charge of the process. This team of people needs to be put into place long before the building is scheduled to start, perhaps a few years beforehand, depending on the circumstances.

Some churches will create two committees: one is often called a long-range planning or vision committee, and the other is usually the building committee. Following this approach, the vision committee usually determines needs and feasibility; deciding what needs to be built and when. In this scenario, the building committee is responsible for the actual hiring of professionals and getting the building built. While this method can and does work, many churches will only use one committee to do it all. In the context of this chapter, unless otherwise noted, I will refer to either or both committees as the building committee, as everything is applicable to either methodology.

Building Committee - Overall Structure

In my experience, there are two methods of running building committees that seem to be the most effective. The first method is a small committee of 3 to 4 people who enjoy a high degree of confidence and support from the congregation and who do most of the work and decision-making. This approach typically works well in smaller churches. The second is a moderate-sized committee that utilizes subcommittees to engage a larger portion of the body in the decision making process.

I wholeheartedly believe that the "executive" team should be as small as possible, and they should form sub-committees, as needed, to assist with various aspects of design. What do not often work well are the two extremes: large executive committees, or a pastor alone calling the shots.

It is best to get a lot of people from within the congregation involved in the planning and building process in order to help build consensus and unity – they just don't all need to be on the building committee! Alexander Hamilton said, *"Men often oppose a thing merely because they have had no agency in planning it, or because it may have been planned by those whom they dislike."* People who are not involved in the process are much more likely to be unduly critical than those who had a part in the process. Said another way, people tend to throw water on other people's ideas but not their own. People in the church need to have ownership of the solution, and the best way to make this happen is to make them part of the process.

While you want to get as many people involved as desire to help, you don't want to put them all on the building committee! The best way to maximize efficiency, build unity, and utilize the skills and enthusiasm of the congregation is usually through a structure that is comprised of an executive building committee and sub-committees.

Each of the members of the executive building committee will chair one or more of the sub-committees. Most of the work is done in sub-committees with recommendations being passed to the building committee for decisions and communication to leadership and other sub-committees.

Structure of the Executive Building Committee

In order to be effective, an executive building committee should typically be comprised of at least three and no more than ten people. In my experience, the most effective committees are typically moderate in size and are usually not more than six or seven people. In this executive committee there should be a chairman, a secretary, and possibly a vice-chairperson. The chairperson (or in their absence, the vice-chair) is responsible for administration and coordination of the building committee and its subcommittees. The secretary's role is primarily to document and communicate while the other member's primary roles are to chair various sub-committees.

The purpose of the executive committee is to assign tasks, receive reports and recommendations from sub-committees, and make recommendations and decisions. They are also to communicate to the church leadership, the congregation, and other professionals hired by the church.

The amount of time and effort required of the executive committee and subcommittees during the planning process is usually lessened by the involvement of an outside resource such as denominational resource, an experienced pastor or lay leader, or 3rd party such as a consultant. *In this book, the term consultant refers to any of those — the resource from outside your church with the experience to help you get from where you are to where you need to be.*

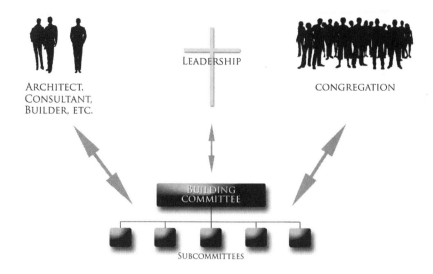

As the church's experienced guide, a consultant can move a building committee through the planning phase more quickly. A consultant can also off-load a significant portion of the analysis from the church, as the consultant will have more experience, better tools, and more resources than the church. Speaking from my own personal experience, it is almost always easier, and certainly faster, for the consultant to do analysis than to teach the church how to do it, guide it through the process, evaluate findings, and then help refine the results.

Using this strategy, the building committee is tasked with data collection which is forwarded to a consultant for analysis and recommendation. The consultant then makes recommendations in a report back to the building committee who will then evaluate and refine the recommendations in conjunction with the consultant. This process alleviates much of the work for a committee that already has its hands full. The resulting recommendations are discussed between the building committee, the leadership, and congregation (as appropriate), and then refined as needed.

Likewise, during the design and construction process, having the right design or construction firm will make the committee's job much easier. In a perfect world, the professionals that work with your church should, in effect, become part of the church team and offload the staff and committees of a great deal of effort and stress.

Staffing Committees

In his book *Courageous Leadership,* Bill Hybels wrote about three C's when it comes to staffing: Character, Competence, and Chemistry. The people on your committee should be evaluated using these criteria in that order. I agree with him that character is by far the most important quality, with competence and then chemistry being the other two primary factors.

Without exception, the men and women who serve on the executive building committee should display the following qualifications and characteristics:

§ Be known and respected by the congregation.

§ Display a life of good Christian character and integrity.

§ Display a servant's heart.

§ Understand and totally support the church vision and mission.

§ Be good listeners and of humble spirit.

§ Be peacemakers and reconcilers.

§ Be faithful financial supporters of the church.

§ Demonstrate good common sense and problem solving skills.

§ Be able to encourage and exhort others.

In short, the people on your executive committee need to be organizers, coaches, and peacemakers who use their time, talents, and treasure for the advancement of the ministry. These skills are much more important than construction or design experience.

It is important to note what qualifications are not significant when selecting the executive building committee team.

⊗ <u>Solely</u> because of being a large financial supporter.

⊗ <u>Solely</u> because of being an elder, deacon, pastor, or otherwise in a church leadership position.

⊗ Being a person of prominence or one who enjoys being in the limelight.

⊗ Just being strong willed and able to get things done.

The scriptures state God gives grace to the humble and resists the proud. Some of the best building committee members are people of quiet strength and humble spirit. While you may have people on the building committee that are large contributors, on staff, or person of prominence, they should not be there *because* of those reasons, but because of their other qualifications.

As for the chairperson of the building committee, that person must truly exemplify all of the above qualifications. Of paramount importance is their walk with God, their dedication to the advancement of the church vision and goals, their communication skills, and their ability to interact with both the leadership and the congregation.

Leading a building program is more spiritual than technical. There is an old saying that when you are a hammer, every problem is a nail, and there is a lot of truth in that. Those in the building industry will always view things through the lens of their personal perspective. Builders or contractors are often not the best planners – that is why they are builders and not architects. Architects frequently have a very narrow viewpoint; all too often it is about the art of design and not functionality or cost. An architect will view the entire project through the lens of their profession, and a builder will do likewise – often with very different views.

To summarize, people involved in the design and construction industry have valuable places in the process; however, *leading* the process *may* not be the best position for many of them.

Subcommittees

As stated earlier, the church may elect to form a vision or planning committee to do research and obtaining church approval to build. It may then form a separate building committee to oversee the actual construction. It is important to think of subcommittees in the context of how the church decides to implement planning and construction in its building program.

Each of the subcommittees is chaired by a member of the executive building committee, with the subcommittees being where the majority of the work is performed. Subcommittees are generally formed for specific purposes and with definite goals and timelines. Upon completion of their assigned tasks, the subcommittee should be dissolved and the members (with the exception of the subcommittee chairperson) be dismissed with thanks, possibly to serve again on another subcommittee. However, some subcommittees such as prayer, legal, financial, and a few others are often formed for the duration of the building program.

Like the executive building committee, larger subcommittees are sometimes composed of a chairperson, a secretary, and some number of members. A subcommittee might have more people on it than the executive committee. If a large number of people wish to serve on a particular subcommittee, it may be advisable to consider an executive group of 3-5 people who are the core of the subcommittee and vote on making recommendations to the building committee. Subcommittees can be further broken down into task groups that report to the subcommittee executive group. The subcommittee executive group would then make recommendations to the executive building committee. Here is a sample list of suggested or potential subcommittees:

Long-term committees

§ Prayer
§ Finance
§ Administration and Timeline
§ Legal
§ Publicity and Communication

Short-term committees

§ Land Search
§ Ministries and Programs
§ Facilities Evaluation and Planning
§ Relocation / Site Evaluation
§ Fixtures and Furnishings
§ Architect Selection
§ Builder Selection
§ Utilities and Maintenance
§ Interior Design
§ Audio/Video/Lighting/Stage Production
§ Sunday School and Christian Education
§ Worker Appreciation/Outreach
§ Landscaping

Each church will have its own needs and its own way of organizing. The key is to try to spread the effort over as large group of people as you can manage so that no one person or group gets burned out during the process.

As stated earlier, an outside resource can usually relieve the church of much of the analysis work. Data collection, communication, and decision making then become the primary tasks of the building committee, while someone with the tools and experience performs the analysis and planning. This strategy allows everyone to do what they are best equipped and gifted to do.

Without going into detail about each of the potential subcommittees, a few are worthy of additional comment.

Finance. Many churches may already have a finance team or finance committee. If so, one or more members of this committee should serve on the finance subcommittee to insure good communication. These people will serve in a dual capacity: to provide good financial information to the building committee for planning purposes, and to monitor spending and budgets during the building process.

Publicity and Communication is a very important committee. Folks get restless when they know something big is happening, but they don't know the details. In the absence of real information, people often invent something to talk about, often without much regard for its accuracy. Communication needs to happen on a regular basis, and it needs to come from a combination of sources including the pulpit, newsletter, website, or bulletin. If there is a slow period in the project, communicate to the congregation that this was anticipated and let them know that the building committee is on top of everything and the project is progressing according to plan.

Prayer. Expanding facilities to do Kingdom work can put your church on the front lines of spiritual battles. From before the church enters into a building program through dedication Sunday, the prayer team must be constantly seeking the guidance, protection, and grace of God. Pray for the building, pray for the leaders and committee members, pray for unity, and pray for those who labor for the church in building the new facility. Set up a prayer schedule to insure that several people are praying each day for the building program.

Worker appreciation and outreach is an evangelistic outreach ministry to those who labor on your building. During construction I strongly urge organizing weekly construction site visits to bring drinks, snacks, and words of thanks and encouragement to the laborers that are building your church.

Your church will want to equip this ministry with gospel tracts and free bibles to hand out. Upon showing up on the job site, the first thing the team should do is pray over the work site and thank God for the workers. Share the food and drink and personally thank as many of the workers as possible. Ask the workers for prayer requests and offer to pray for and with the workers.

By showing the love of Christ to these workers, you will open doors of opportunity to share the Gospel. This ministry will make a great impression on those who are fortunate enough to work on your facility, and the church will have a wonderful chance to sow seed and reap souls for the Kingdom.

Chapter 4 - The Crucial Role of Vision in Building

"You've got to be very careful if you don't know where you are going, because you might not get there." – *Yogi Berra*

When we talk "process" in building, it must first be acknowledged that it all begins with vision. A church building program must start with understanding the God-given vision and mission of the church ministry. A church needs to know where it's going with its building program and why.

Vision and mission provide both the starting point and the direction for your efforts; they are the dual lenses through which a myriad of future decisions must be evaluated.

If vision charts the course for growth, the church needs to insure what it is planning to build is God's vision (destination) for the church. Psalm 127:1 tells us, "*Unless the LORD builds the house, they labor in vain who build it.*" The church need not labor in vain by building something other than His vision for your church.

> To be truly successful, the church must ensure that it is God's vision and timing that is to be accomplished and not their own.

The fundamental missions of the church is to both edify the saints and to win souls for the Kingdom (Eph 4:11-13). The church needs to understand the vision for the church as it pertains to what God has called it to accomplish both within the congregation and the community.

Vision is what the church will be when it *grows up*. It may be helpful to consider the church's **vision** as the destination of what the ministry is called to be, and the church's **mission** as the goals and outcomes that are accomplished in becoming the vision. This reinforces the concept of vision as a destination.

The word *destination* is a noun derived from the word destiny. God's vision for the church should be the church's destination – the church's destiny. The church's goal, supported by every member, should be to become the vision that God has for the church and accomplishing the mission along the way. Mission is what we do - vision is what we become.

> The first step in building is to spend a great deal of time in prayer seeking wisdom and understanding about vision and timing.

One thing no outsider can probably tell you is God's will and His timing for your church's building program. Vision comes from the appointed leadership of the church as they spend time in prayer seeking the will of the Heavenly Father. With respect to timing, sometimes our fleshly thoughts tell us to move forward when we have not heard from God. We can complete the house, but if it is not in God's will or timing, then our considerable labor is in vain. Conversely, there are times when it would seem impossible when God tells us to move forward. Over the years, I've seen miracles happen when godly men and women were sure in their hearts that God was calling them to move forward against the odds.

The Burden of Vision

Vision can sometimes be a terrible burden. God may provide a vision without the context of the time it will take to become the vision. Sometimes church leaders feel that because they have a vision, it must happen quickly.

I am reminded of Joseph and the vision he had from God. I wonder how often Joseph sat in that jail cell expecting to be delivered at any moment, when it was going to be 10 years or more until he was free and God's revealed vision began to manifest itself. What a long time and much preparation between vision and the working out of the vision! Wisdom would dictate that we prepare to do what we can when we can, and then wait on the Lord and His timing to bring the vision to fruition.

Many times vision comes to pass in a measured fashion, such as when God gave Moses the vision of the Promised Land. He told Moses that He would not go before him in a year and wipe the land clean, but He would do it "*by little and little... until thou be increased, and inherit the land.*" In other words, they were going to get what they needed <u>when they needed it</u>. Paul said, "*God will meet all your needs according to His riches in Jesus Christ.*" He never said all your wants! Stated perhaps a bit more poetically, albeit less grammatically correct, God promised to meet your needs, not your greeds. God's will in His timing will get His provision. I fully recognize that this is certainly easier to say than it is to live out on a daily basis, but it is nonetheless true for that.

When the Vision is Bigger Than The Budget

God's vision for your church may be far larger than its budget. That is not only okay - it is what you should often expect! The One and True Living God is a God of growth. God's vision for Israel, as they were led out of Egypt to occupy the Promised Land, was more than they could ever have hoped to accomplish within their own abilities. God was faithful to progressively deliver the promised vision as Israel developed both the need for the land and the ability to maintain the land. (Of course Israel had that little obedience problem that interfered with the timing of the promise, but that's another story.) If you have a God-given vision that exceeds your ability, the vision will most likely be realized in phases as the church grows and has the ability to support that growth.

Over the years I have spoken with a countless number pastors firm in their conviction they had a vision from God for a facility many times what they could possibly afford. It is not my place to tell someone what the Lord may have laid on their heart. But I have seen almost every one of those churches fail to achieve the vision because they wanted the whole Promised Land at once instead of little by little.

> If you have a need, build what you can afford. As God gives the increase you will be able to afford the next phase of the vision.

Don't make the mistake of thinking you have to build the whole vision at once! Churches that overreach often find themselves with financial pressures that can have a negative impact on ministry. Jesus tells us in Luke 14 that a man is to count the cost to know whether he has enough to finish. Jesus did not say to build beyond what the builder could accomplish, but to insure that he (the builder) could finish it in his own ability. As God gives the increase, the church will be empowered to grow into the vision He has provided. If God unexpectedly opens the gates of heaven and pours out His financial blessings on the church, it is able to move into the next phase perhaps quicker than planned. If not, the church is able to make the payments in its own ability and will be ready when He gives the increase.

A tightly held vision is ineffective. Habakkuk 2:2 states it this way, *"Then the LORD answered me and said: 'Write the vision and make it plain on tablets, that he may run who reads it.'"* If only the pastor or a handful of people share the vision, there is no power of agreement in unity. To be effective, vision must be:

§ Clearly and repeatedly communicated in several different ways.

§ Be understood by the congregation - they need to understand it the way the leaders do.

§ Embraced by the congregation - it has to become their vision.

§ Able to provoke a response from the members of the church.

If God has a vision or mission for the church that is not being accomplished, then something needs to be done about it. James said it this way in verse 17 of Chapter 4, *"Therefore, to him who knows to do good and does not do it, to him it is sin."*

> If there is a God-given vision and mission that is not being accomplished because of building or land issues, it should be clear to the congregation there is a _need_ to build.

At this point, building becomes more than just an idea, more than just a want or desire - *it is a call to action to meet a Kingdom need.* The concept of need is very important. For the most part, the membership will not support a building plan unless they personally understand and agree with the *need* to build.

It all starts or fails with vision. God said His people are destroyed for lack of vision, and while it may not kill you, a lack of clear vision can hinder or even cripple a building program. Psalms 127 teaches us that building man's vision is a waste of time, and Proverbs 16:9 reminds us that, *"A man's heart plans his way, but the LORD directs his steps."* Church leaders need to get into their prayer closets and determine His will and timing to build and allow God to direct their steps. When *you know that you know that you know*, the church can then get on with the rest of the process.

Remember: What the church decides to build must be examined through the lenses of God's vision and His mission for the church. Sometimes it turns out that what the church <u>needs</u> to build is not exactly what the leadership or congregation <u>desires</u> to build. If this is the case in your church, remember the words of Jesus in His prayer, *"Yet not my will, but Yours, be done."*

The Benefits of Outside Counsel

Scripture tells us there is safety in the counsel of many. In fact, this quotation from Proverbs 24 is on the front cover of this book as an exhortation to find that safety. Whether from an experienced pastor, a denominational resource, or an outside consultant, the church will benefit from help in objectively analyzing its needs and abilities. A person from outside the church family has no personal agenda and is outside the politics and peer influences of the church membership. An outside influence will not avoid sacred cow issues and can be helpful in generating new ideas that may not occur to the membership just because "we've never done it that way before".

Following an objective impartial finding of fact, an outside resource can make a recommendation to the church that is objective, free of partisan influence, and is based on a wide range of church building experience.

Another important point to consider is that someone from outside your church will see things more the way visitors will. By that I mean people who have been attending the church for years do not see the building or facilities in the same way that a visitor does. When I was a manager of a computer retail store, one of my mentors told me that it is very hard to see your store the way customers do. My problem was similar to that of most church members; because of familiarity, I saw my surroundings more in my mind than with my eyes. I might add that the picture we have in our mind's eye is often a lot rosier than reality.

True Story: A church had been debating for years on what to build with no success. While they were on a major street and one of the few churches in their area serving their demographic, they were not growing. A couple of the observations I made were, that the church was hard to see from the road, and the poor maintenance of the building would give a negative view as to the character of the church - that is, the church and the people were not really old and decrepit. I took pictures and used them in our presentation to help the saints realize just what people really saw from the street and when they approached the church. It was a matter of only a few weeks before many of those issues, which had existed for years, were addressed. Today it looks very different and certainly sends a different message to visitors. As a result of a needs and feasibility study, the church accomplished more in 6 weeks than it had in the previous 5 years and they have a plan with which to continue to move forward with their building program

Through repetitive exposure, a congregation will grow blind to conditions and issues that a consultant (and visitors) may see plainly. Think about it this way, have you ever been somewhere and noticed a strong odor that seemed to fade away until you left the room and came back? The odor did not fade; your nose (actually your brain) got used to it and subtracted it from your conscious thought. In much the same way, our mind gets used to things being a certain way and can subtract them from our mental picture. This causes us to see things differently than visitors do.

Almost without exception, the church will greatly benefit from an outside viewpoint and experienced assistance with tactical issues, including those of understanding need, financial ability, and plan development. The reason I am so adamant about this is because I have seen church after church heading down a bad path, spending money they did not need to spend, failing in building programs that did not need to fail, losing unity in the body of Christ, and churches even splitting because of poor planning and execution. I have seen good men and women beaten up by the building process and chased away from further service or even leaving the church, including pastors stepping down from the pulpit.

Your church is about to embark on a commercial development project that will cost hundreds of thousands or millions of dollars. Mistakes can easily cost tens of thousands of dollars and will negatively impact the church's overall satisfaction with the building project or even hinder its effectiveness in ministry. In the worse case, it can set the church back years or even split the church. *Before you recoil at the perceived cost of engaging wise counsel, it is imperative to understand the risk and to count the potential cost of mistakes.*

As an associate expressed it, "Inexperience leads to gaps in knowledge. Gaps in knowledge lead to mistakes. Mistakes cost money." There you have it, about as succinct and clear as anyone could hope to ask.

Investment in wise counsel is just that, an investment. An investment is something that is expected to be recouped with an increase. Ben Franklin said it well when he was quoted as saying, "*An investment in knowledge always pays the best interest.*"

It is important to understand that a lack of experience puts you in the position that you don't know what you don't know. Outside council can provide the experience to ask the right questions and the objective viewpoint to help the church separate needs and wants. *The investment in expert help pays multiple dividends in time, money, and reduced effort.*

Summary of Benefits from Outside Counsel

§ Able to provide a proven and objective process that will save the church time, stress, and effort.

§ Has a broad base of church construction experience that can help provide a better solution at a lower cost.

§ Is not <u>unduly</u> influenced by history or a vocal minority.

§ Can serve as a lightning rod for critical comments to help maintain unity in the body.

§ Can be an arbitrator and peacemaker to help maintain unity in the body and protect the leadership.

§ Often has access to resources that the church does not.

§ Translates ministry needs and wants into building and land requirements.

§ Can save your church many times the cost of their fees which *often makes all of the above benefits essentially free.*

In the final analysis, an investment in wise counsel should cost you nothing, in fact, quite the contrary; it should save you money! This is the difference between a cost and an investment. When the concern is about the cost of wise counsel, it is important to realize that money is going to be spent anyway, either in wise counsel or in additional effort and mistakes that result in reduced efficiency and a higher project cost. You get to pick!

Separating Needs & Wants

As we have previously discussed, building your church begins with vision. The *vision highlights and defines the <u>need</u> to build.* Said another way, when the building (or lack thereof) becomes a stumbling block to ministry, this defines a quantifiable need to build. The problem is that if fifty people are asked their opinion of what they *think* the church needs to build, the church would probably get more than fifty different answers because some of them are double minded! This is why congregational surveys are only one facet of a needs analysis. As a consultant, one of my favorite quotes is by Henry Ford that deals with giving people what they think they want, *"If I'd asked my customers what they wanted, they'd have said a faster horse."* Where would we be today without his vision to buck the trend by addressing needs rather than wants? Wants very seldom walk hand in hand with needs.

One of the many difficulties the church must overcome is that of separating and prioritizing needs and wants. As imperfect, fallible humans, we often think the ministries or programs in which we are personally involved are more important or deserving than others; it's just human nature. This often makes the process of prioritization difficult to do *objectively* when you are a member of that church.

Over the years I have talked to many church leaders about building. A vast majority of them talk about building in terms of what they *want* to build. A much smaller group talks about what they *need* to build. Not to split hairs, but I believe it is more than just a matter of semantics, it's a matter of providence. God has promised to meet our needs and not our wants. When preparing to build, the church's needs and wants must be identified and then prioritized. I have noticed that, in many cases, churches were able to afford what was needed but struggled with affording what they wanted. Sometimes this struggle to afford wants has delayed a building program for years.

True Story: A number of years ago I was contacted by a church that was looking for help. They explained that about 4 years previously they had a set of plans drawn for their church that would have cost $1,200,000 to build. The problem was the church could only afford a $700,000 project. Now, I could stop right here and make the point that this church was in trouble because they did not take the time to properly prepare for a building program, but I won't – because the story gets even better, I mean worse.

The church decided that instead of scaling the building program to what they could afford, they would raise the $500,000 shortfall. They executed a capital campaign and did indeed raise the $500,000 over the next 3 years. It was then nearly 5 years since they originally designed their building. When they went back to the builders to get updated pricing on the project, they found the estimated cost had risen to over $1,700,000. They were heartbroken to learn that after nearly 5 years and incredible financial sacrifice, they were nearly $100,000 *further* away from their project than when they started. Sadly, there was nothing I could do for them except tell them to do what they should have done 5 years before, and that was to scale the building project down to their budget.

Note: The cost increases in this real life example were not out of line or even unusual in a growing economy. Generally speaking, construction costs go up between 6% and 10% per year. Their average cost increase of $500,000 over 5 years on a $1.2M program was slightly over 8% annually – right in the middle of the normal range.

Now it is time for me return from that rabbit trail and continue our discussion of *need*. As stated earlier, land and facility *issues that hinder* the church from achieving its vision and mission *define the need* to build. For example, let's say the church has more than adequate sanctuary space but too few classrooms and the vision and mission of the church are to create discipled families by reaching children and families through Christian education and family counseling. People visit the church but find the lack of adequate Sunday school or nursery space to be a stumbling block to continued attendance. The vision and mission define the need to build additional classrooms and/or multi-purpose rooms, and the fact visitors are not returning members because of this space issue verify the need. Properly done, new space will meet the worship, educational, fellowship, counseling, and other ancillary ministry needs in order to accomplish the mission and help the church become the vision.

In order to create a long-term master plan, one must quantify the amount and type of space that can be built within the constraints of the budget, and what effect adding this space might have on future sanctuary needs. The church must always plan beyond the current phase and always be looking ahead to make sure the decisions implemented now won't haunt the church in the future.

One might well pose the question, "why can't an architect do this?" A few can, but many do not know enough about church to be the most effective designer, and I have yet to meet an architect that would (or was qualified) help with the church's budgeting to determine what the church could afford. Too few have the inclination, ability, or experience to effectively assist the church in ministry space planning. Mark my words; there is a lot of difference between an architect and a church architect.

All too often the first question out of the architect's mouth is, "what do you want to build?" This question immediately puts the design process into the realm of the subjective instead of the objective – and it is the reason that the vast majority of churches end up with a design that is two, three, or even four times what the church can afford.

> **Think about it…** Call me silly, but it seems unwise to let someone who derives financial benefit in proportion to the size and cost of the building project determine by their design the size and cost of the project!

Sadly, an additional reason that some architects do not provide this service is that since most architectural firms get paid to draw and they get paid whether you build or not. You may find this hard to believe, but more than one architect has made the statement that the best plans they ever designed were the ones that never got built. Why? Because they got paid but never had to deal with the issues of actually getting the building built – they did not have to deal with the builder or inspectors, or deal with any of the issues that come up in the course of a building program.

What the church *needs* to build is objectively quantified by understanding the needs of each of its programs and ministries, how they have grown to this point, and then projecting how they may grow to become the vision and accomplish the mission. The church also needs to identify programs and ministries that do not exist today due to lack of space, budget, or staffing limitations, but are expected to be part of the future church.

The old saying of making the shoe fit the foot is very applicable in this circumstance - you need to make sure the building is made to fit the ministry and not the other way around. The process of design should be one of molding the building around the needs of the ministries instead of trying to make ministries fit into a plan that looks good.

In the soul searching phase of determining needs and wants, the church must ask and answer the questions if it really even needs to build, and if so, why. I think it important to define the word *need*. I believe that in order to depend on a Kingdom provision to meet the need, the need must be defined as a Kingdom need. A Kingdom need is something that must be done in order to accomplish the mission and become the vision that God has for your church.

Chapter 5 - Design

According to the US Census Bureau, the annual value of church construction in 2009 was approximately 6.2 billion dollars. On average, most architects will charge between 6-7% of the project cost on architectural and engineering. Six percent of six billion dollars is $360,000,000 spent each year on design – and **this is just the expense for projects that actually get built!** For every set of church plans that gets built, there are several that do not. Recall the story in Chapter 1 where 20 of 22 pastors in a room had a set of plans that had never been built? Many churches do not build the first set of plans; some don't build the 2nd set either! There are untold *millions of dollars wasted every year* by churches on plans that they cannot build because of poor planning. Please do not become part of this statistic.

When churches seriously begin to consider building, the majority start by developing plans too early in the process. As demonstrated in Chapter 1, there is a lot of work to do before signing on the dotted line with an architect or builder.

If your church enters into the design process without having objectively determined its ministry driven space needs, what it can afford to build based on actual financial ability, and what the land will support, you must back up and complete those steps. Failure to do so will almost certainly cost your church time, money, and good will in the design process. Refer to appendix 'A' in the back of this book for a readiness assessment to determine how ready your church is to build.

Successful church design is based on:

§ Vision

§ Needs

§ Financial ability

§ Site feasibility

The church's future vision is most often bigger than its current need or financial ability. Vision sets the overall framework for what the church designs; it becomes the framework within which we evaluate the other factors of needs, financial ability, and site feasibility.

Future vision is the canvas on which we diagram the interaction of the fundamental defining factors between need and both financial and land feasibility. As the following diagram illustrates, ***the proper design solution lies in the region where all the defining factors are properly accommodated.***

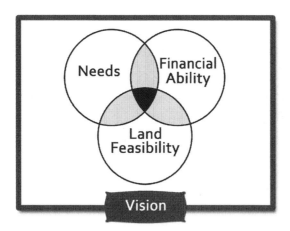

While the process of design needs to be sensitive to the history and culture of the church, it must be steadfastly and primarily focused meeting the *future* needs of the ministry. The inventor Charles Kettering had this to say of the future, "*My interest is in the future because*

I am going to spend the rest of my life there." It is important to remember that the church you build today is not so much for the current membership as it is for those yet to come. The goal in church design should be to develop a set of plans that will meet the church's current and future functional needs within the financial ability of the church. Properly done, the process will produce a design the church can afford that provides balanced space and future expansion options.

By balanced space, I refer to a design that at some future time, when the sanctuary is 75 percent full, the classrooms are 75 percent full, the parking lot is 75 percent full, and you can still find a place to sit for a chicken dinner in the fellowship hall. Balanced space makes the most effective use of every construction dollar as space is not wasted or underutilized.

While a balanced space plan is seldom 100% accurate in meeting future needs (after all, no man knows the future), the only way to get close to it is through an *objective* understanding of the historic growth of the church, its current needs, and a reasoned projection of future need. This will help the church create a space requirements plan to drive the architectural process.

When architectural plans are started without this objective understanding of need, financial ability, or vision, the church design can *only* be driven by *subjective* criteria such as appearance, style, or an unqualified opinion (an opinion based on something other than factual data). **The most common result of a subjective process is a set of architectural plans that do not effectively meet the real needs or budget of the church.**

All too often the leadership, building committee, or church body places too much focus on the appearance of the building and not enough on the function. Once the functionality and space requirements have been determined, the church can, within reason, design the building to look however it wants.

After reading this far, it should not come as a surprise that the design of the new church facility must be driven by the following factors:

Vision: What is God's vision for your church? What is the church going to be when it grows up?

Mission: What is the church trying to accomplish for the community and congregation?

Financial Ability: What can the church afford to build and how will it be paid for?

Needs: What does the church *need* to build in order to become the vision and accomplish the mission?

Land: Is it feasible to build on the land? Will the land support the vision of the church or even the next phase of development?

The design for what is built, whether it is the church's first building, relocation, or an expansion to the current campus, must focus on helping the ministry to become the vision. The long-term vision for the church's ministry is often accomplished in phases. It is often wise to develop a master plan that conceptually shows each phase and the order in which the church expects to build those phases.

Do not spend more than necessary on conceptual master site plans as they are seldom built exactly as proposed. If a master plan is needed for visioning or for the fundraising, only pay for as much detail as is required to communicate the vision. Early in the process the church will typically only need conceptual drawings. Conceptual drawings have fundamental information showing spatial relationships, dimensions, and descriptive text, but do not have the detail needed to actually build. This is an adequate level of detail in to communicate vision to the congregation, support fundraising, and have a preliminary plan review with the city. The cost for this level of detail is generally about 25% of the cost of complete construction drawings. Construction drawings are needed to develop accurate cost estimates, obtain a loan, obtain building permits, and of course, to build.

Options for conceptual plans in order of increasing cost:

1. Single Line Drawing
2. Shaded Drawing
3. Color Drawing
4. Full-color, Photo-realistic Artist's Rendering
5. Computerized 3D Model with Walk-through
6. Scale Model

How much should be spent on conceptual plans and how much is too much? That is something each church will have to decide based on the value received from the conceptual plans.

The Benefits of Conceptual Master Planning

§ Provides a clear vision to help create unity and focus by clarifying the need to build.

§ Helps the congregation develop a comfort level that the leadership has a long-term plan for achieving church goals.

§ Insures the early stages of the building program do not become a hindrance to future phases.

§ Forces the church to think through a long-term plan.

§ Provides a key component of a capital stewardship campaign.

§ Provides a plan to take to the city or county to insure that the church's concept is reasonable and feasible given the local zoning, land use codes, utilities, and access.

§ Insures you have enough land to accomplish the vision and mission.

Each phase of the church's master plan should have clear and quantifiable goals. For instance: sanctuary seating for 300, classrooms for 50 elementary age children, fellowship hall for 200, and so on. As we have said several times, *what the church designs must reflect the needs of the ministries while being in balance with what the church can afford.* The dual processes of determining both need and financial ability provide the foundation for the design phase of the church facilities. That is so important I am going to repeat it.

> The dual processes of determining *both* need and financial ability provide the foundation for the design of the church facilities.

It is important, whenever possible, not to attempt to make the foot fit the shoe but to make the building meet the needs and abilities of the ministry. A thorough understanding of the needs of the ministries and the financial abilities of the church are required in order to count the cost. (Sound familiar yet?)

Important Concept: Financial analysis determines the scope (size) of your project. A needs analysis determines how that space is designed to best meet ministry needs.

A proper design process, viewed as a series of steps, will minimize risk by:

1. Defining need and what should be built to meet the need.

2. Developing a conceptual master site plan to insure the long-term project is viable.

3. Developing conceptual plans for the current building phase to increase congregational support.

4. Determining rough preliminary construction estimates based on the conceptual plans to insure the church does not invest heavily in a project it cannot afford.

Things to Remember in the Design Process:

§ Contract only for the services needed at that stage of the process (for instance conceptual drawings) and give the vendor an opportunity to earn more of the church's business (i.e. construction drawings) later. Make sure there is a way for the church to terminate the agreement at certain milestones should it be decided not to move forward with the building program, if the architect or engineer does not perform to your satisfaction, or a decision is made to use another design professional for any other reason.

§ The same principle applies to design/build as it does to architectural and engineering services. Do not sign a development agreement with a design/build firm without the right to cancel at the end of either conceptual or working drawings without undue expense. The church needs to reasonably compensate the design team or builder for expenses incurred to that point, but make sure you understand what the walk-away costs and liabilities are at any point.

§ Do not bypass good process for any reason. Know what the church needs and can afford to build (see counting the cost) before engaging any design professional.

§ Talk to the local planning or building department before getting too far into the design process. It is a free venue in which to discuss ideas and make sure that the local governing authority has no issue with your ideas before spending a lot of money on plans that cannot be built.

§ Look for a design professional or design/build firm that regularly designs *churches* of the *type, style, and price range* the church needs to build. Just because a design professional may have designed a couple of multi-million dollar churches does not mean they would be the best choice for an $800,000 project.

When shopping for architects, pay special attention to how they calculate fees. A fixed-price contract for each phase of services is usually a good pricing model. A fixed-price contract that includes price protection for reasonable corrections, errors, and omissions relieves the church of financial uncertainty in the design process. In practice, paying a fixed price per square foot of designed space is the safest and fairest pricing model, as opposed to the architect charging a percentage of the building cost.

Important Concept: A percentage-based fee provides no incentive for the architect to save the church money in the design or building process; in fact, one can easily make the case that the opposite is true. A percentage-based design agreement is more likely to be an encouragement to increase the cost of your project because the designer will make more money. In a percentage-based contract for services, your financial goals and those of the architect or builder can be in opposition since they make less money when they save you money.

Questions to Ask When Hiring an Architect

The design and construction of church facilities may very well be one of the most important activities in your organization's history. One of the many critical components of your building success is hiring the right architect. The church must consider bids from architects or design/build firms who have a good reputation for building churches of the type and style you are considering and are familiar with designing within the budget range the church can afford.

General Background Questions

1. How long has the architect been in business?

2. What percentage of the firm's business is designing church facilities?

3. Does the architect commonly do church projects of the style, size, and budget the church anticipates building?

4. When and what was the architect's most recent project?

5. When and where was the architect's most current project similar to yours?

6. What is the proposed mediation process for resolving disputes and will the architect agree to handle disputes through Christian arbitration?

Proposed Project Questions

1. How well does the architect understand the church's goals and constraints? (Ask the architect to reiterate back to you the overall goals, design, and budget constraints, and evaluate how well they understand them.)

2. What is the objective process that the architect will use to gather information for evaluating the needs and goals of the ministry to provide the optimum design solution?

3. What experience does the architect have for translating ministry needs into space requirements?

4. How viable does the architect believe your proposed project is with respect to timeline, budget, and land constraints?

Fees & Contractual Issues

1. How does the architect establish fees and when will payments be expected?

2. How does the architect tie fee payments to milestones or phases in the scope of work?

3. What are the architectural and engineering fees for each phase of this project?

4. What specific services do the fees cover?

5. How does the architect establish fees for additional services?

6. How does the architect establish fees for reimbursable expenses?

7. If consultants or engineers (civil, structural, mechanical, electrical, geotechnical, testing, etc.) are necessary, are their fees included in the architect's quoted fee or are they separate services?

8. How might the church structure the contract so that the church has the ability to walk away from the agreement at the conclusion of any phase without additional cost or penalty?

9. What is the architect's markup on third party services if they sub-contract a portion of the work?

10. Will the architect provide construction cost estimates for the project?

11. What happens if the architect's construction estimates are grossly out of line with construction quotes?

12. Who is liable for the cost of redesign if it is necessary to meet the construction budget?

13. Will there be additional charges for changes required by the building department or other government agency? If so, how are these charges calculated?

14. How are additional charges computed for design changes requested by the church after working drawings are already completed?

15. How are additional charges computed for design changes requested by the contractor?

16. Who is financially responsible for correcting errors and omissions in design and bids?

Making the Final Decision

Do not trust your feelings, check the references! Call or visit each reference that each architect gives you and ask and evaluate the answers to the following questions:

1. How well did the architect adhere to schedules?

2. How well did the architect live up to the expectations they set during the sales process?

3. Did the project complete within budget? If not, why not?

4. Were the references pleased with the architect's services and their working relationship with the architect? (Compare to the architect's explanation to the same question.)

5. Did the architect listen to their concerns and attempt to resolve them to their satisfaction?

6. Would the reference hire the architect again? Why or why not?

7. What problems surfaced during the project?

8. What were the architect's strong points?

9. What were the architect's weak points?

10. What would the reference do differently next time with respect to the project design and working with the architect?

Ask each reference about other projects they know with which the architect was or has since been involved. This will give some additional references to check. Remember, no one will knowingly hand out references that will not give a glowing report. Seeking out other "off list" references may give a more balanced viewpoint.

Subjective Issues to Evaluate and Consider

These are questions that may not always be directly asked but may be evaluated from the architect's responses to other questions and actions.

1. How interested is the architect in the project?

2. How much time and effort has the architect put into winning the church's business and earning their confidence?

3. What sets this architect apart from the rest?

4. How well does the architect respond to being asked why he or she should be hired over someone else?

5. How well do your thoughts on why this architect may be the best fit for the church line up with their answer on why you should hire them?

6. On other projects, how well has the architect performed in bringing projects to completion within the proposed budget?

7. How well does the architect understand the church's goals, priorities, and constraints?

8. Is the architect's personality a good fit with the church?

9. Are the agreements and pricing for services straightforward and easy to understand?

10. Has the architect responded to the church's questions and communications in a timely and accurate fashion?

It is recommended that a form (or forms) be created with all the questions and which provides space for ranking replies which permits each person on the evaluation team to rank each vendor response on a scale of 1 to 10.

If possible, visit the projects the architect has used as references for their services and, if possible, speak to members of the building committee. This will provide an objective valuation for each applicant that should weigh heavily in the final decision and help eliminate personal feelings and preferences.

As you may notice, many of the questions assume the church has a good idea of what it wants to build, why there is a need to build, and what it can afford. If these questions have not been objectively and definitively answered, it is very likely premature to solicit the services of an architect or design/build firm.

Pre-developed or Stock Church Plans

A viable option that warrants consideration is that of working with an architectural firm that provides pre-developed or pre-engineered plans in addition to developing custom designed plans.

The church may be able to save a great deal of time and money on church building plans by using pre-engineered or stock church plans. These plans are from another church building program that can be modified for this church's building project.

Besides having a distinct price advantage, these plans have the additional benefit of having already been built, the costs are known, and the design kinks worked out. Using this design approach, the church uses the results of its needs and feasibility study to look at an architect's catalog of church plans for a specific size and style of building plan that meets its criteria. This enables the church to get its plans for less cost and to typically get them faster than having them drawn completely from scratch.

Most likely, the church will not find a church plan that is in *perfect* alignment with the church's needs. However, plans that are reasonably close can be easily modified to rearrange, within reason, the internal structure and most exterior features of the building. Changes such as resizing rooms and moving rooms can typically be done with minimal time and cost. Many plans will support the addition of a basement or even a balcony. If the church finds a plan that is exciting and can be adapted to meet their criteria, it can save a great deal of money and a lot of time by using a stock plan modified to its needs.

In summary, the use of stock plans will typically cut many weeks off the design process while reducing the cost of church design. It is also important to note that a catalog of church building plans can also be a great catalyst for stimulating a church building committee's thinking and excitement. Just make sure that the plans are provided and sealed by an architect licensed in the state in which they will be used.

A final word of caution: Picking a plan out of a catalog without the objective understanding of what you need and can afford is just as much a recipe for failure as creating custom plans with the same lack of understanding. Know what you need, why you need it, what you can afford, and how you will pay for it before getting excited about any church plan.

Chapter 6 - Financing

In the past, some churches found financing church construction was a relatively easy task while for others it was a source of seemingly never-ending frustration. In the post-2008 economy, most churches find themselves closer to the never-ending frustration end of the curve. If your church has not attempted a loan since 2008, you are in for a different, and probably not so pleasant, experience.

Lending is much more difficult for the church than at any time in recent memory and that is not likely to change much in the next few years. As I said in one of my seminars, it's a whole new ball game and churches must relearn the rules.

Common Financing Misconceptions & Mistakes

Misconception: *"We've never had a problem with financing before."* Many churches today do not understand how much smaller the lending market has become and how much more difficult the borrowing process will be. As of this writing, many of the larger lenders no longer finance church construction. This means there is a smaller pool of potential lenders, and for the most part those remaining lenders also have less money available for mortgage loans. The result is the church has to compete for loans from a smaller pool of lenders with less money, and the lenders will cherry pick who they lend to. Due to increased lending regulation, the loan process will take longer, require a higher level of documentation, and will probably result in a lower percentage of the project being funded than the church anticipates.

Misconception: *"The bank knows we are good for it."* Lenders essentially want to see the church making the mortgage payment to itself before they will lend it the money. They are not going to take your word on future increased giving or potential changes to expenses. If you are borrowing a million dollars, the working assumption is that you can show a history of putting about $8,000 per month away into savings in order to prove you can make the mortgage payment.

Mistake: The church overestimates how much of the project cost the lender will finance. Pre-2008, some lenders would provide 100% financing, up to 80% of the value of the improved assets. Essentially, if you had any significant assets in land or buildings, you might have borrowed 100% of the project costs – but no more! Today, you will find most lenders financing between 65% and 75% of the value of assets *and* they will often want the church to have cash in the project, not just land and building equity.

Mistake: The church overestimates the power of assets. Too frequently, churches proceed under the assumption that the bank will loan them money based on their assets. Equity (assets) alone is insufficient to qualify your church for a loan. While a lack of equity will kill a loan deal, assets alone will not make the deal. Just because your church has land and buildings worth $1M – don't expect to be able to borrow $1M.

Misconception: Another incorrect assumption is the church can qualify for a loan based on its projected future revenue, whether from church growth or from a proposed Christian daycare or school. In some cases, where the church has an existing daycare or school and a backlog of enrollments, the lender *may* consider some portion of this projected future revenue in qualifying the church for a loan. Otherwise, you will find the lender deaf, dumb, and blind to claims of future revenue or financial growth.

Financial Ability & Counting the Cost

"For which of you, intending to build a tower does not sit down first and count the cost, whether he has enough to finish it." (Luke 14:28)

Before the church begins to work with an architect or design/build firm to develop floor plans, and certainly before hiring a builder, it must be understood what the church can afford - it must first count the cost.

The parable of counting the cost before building was obviously not intended as a command on how to build. Jesus used it as a truism to demonstrate a common sense approach (dare we say, a proper process!) to illustrate a Kingdom truth. For our purposes, we want to focus on the truism that one must count the cost before one builds.

J. Oswald Sanders had this to say about the above verse in his book *Shoe Leather Commitment*, "Jesus employed these illustrations to demonstrate His disapproval of impulsive and ill-considered discipleship. Like the builder, He too is engaged in a building program – *'On this rock, I will build my church.'*"

When Christ admonishes us to first count the cost of building, by implication there must have been some prior action. Why is this? Because one cannot count the cost of the unknown! This biblical example of counting the cost actually breaks down into a 4-step process

First it would need to be determined that something needed to be built. The building was contemplated because there was a need that was not being met.

Secondly, the builder would determine where to build. He would need to decide whether to build on the plain or on the mountainside. The builder would build where it would best meet his needs. Building on the side of a mountain might aptly meet the needs of a goat farmer, but would not best meet the needs of the builder who was a farmer.

And believe me, it's a lot cheaper to build on flat land than try to hang a church on the side of a mountain!

Thirdly, the builder had to determine whether to build a tower or another type of building. This is the second step of making the building meet the need. He knows where to build, and now he answers the question of what he needs to build, at least in a broad sense of defining the general characteristics of the building.

And finally, in the fourth step the builder, having defined the type of building needed, would further refine it as to whether he needed a 3-story tower, a 10-story tower, or Trump Tower, as defined by the budget and need. Once again, the builder is crafting the tool to fit the problem rather than making the problem fit the tool. Your building should fit the ministry, not the ministry fit the building.

In short, the builder needed to understand his need to build, where he wanted to build, and what he needed to build. Once that was done, *then* the cost could be counted to see if there was enough to finish, to insure what was planned was within his ability to pay. It is also important to understand Jesus did not say whether He (God the Father) has enough to finish it, he was referring to he the builder.

We all recognize there is a fine line between faith and foolishness. Prudence would dictate that in most circumstances the church should build what it knows it can afford and not build solely on potentially misplaced faith. I realize this statement may not sit well with some readers, but too often we all (not just churches in building programs) plan first and pray later; we ask God to bless our mess, which is nothing short of prideful presumption on our part. If the church is building God's vision in His timing, then moving forward in faith is not misplaced. **If the church is moving forward with any other vision or timing, then there is no *valid* basis for faith.**

When the church builds based on what they know they can afford, and God then opens the gates of heaven and pours additional financial blessing on the church, the church is in a position to move into its next phase of building quickly. Conversely, if the church builds on projected financial growth that does not happen, then the church will be left in financial duress with a project that it cannot afford.

> Once you understand the vision and mission, you must then determine how much of that vision you can afford to build today.

The proper way to approach design is for the church to first determine its actual needs and financial ability, and then design a building that meets its needs within its budget.

Plan, budget, and then design; what a concept! It seems like common sense, but it is surprising the number of churches that plan, design, and then budget, or even worse, design and then budget with little or no real planning.

Estimating a Maximum Building Budget

You maximum building budget defined as: the cash the church has on hand now, plus the cash that can be raised in contributions by the end of construction (other than loans), plus cash from the sale of assets, plus the amount of money that can be borrowed through loans or bonds. This total equals the maximum building budget.

The purpose of this exercise is to set an optimistic upper limit for the building budget. Using this total, the church will get the first approximation of the maximum possible budget for the building program.

The following chart illustrates the simple 4-part equation to develop a preliminary building budget.

Cash on Hand	
+ Cash Raised by End of Construction	
+ Cash from the Sale of Assets	
+ Financing (Loan or Bonds)	
= Total Estimated Building Budget	

Lending – What to Expect

With the economic upheaval of 2008 came a whole new set of lending challenges. Today, even churches with long histories of good relationships with their lender are surprised and dismayed by the difficulty, and sometimes impossibility, of getting the financing they need. What they are experiencing is the new church lending paradigm that has come into effect since the bank failures from the economic crisis. The rules have changed and we may not see the church-friendly lending environment of pre-2008 for a very long time.

Intellectually, churches understand lending has become more difficult, but many still do not understand how much church lending has fundamentally changed since the fall of 2008, and are therefore unprepared when they approach the lender.

The reasons or justifications as to why many lenders no longer make church loans are unimportant, as the effect is the same – fewer places to find money with which to build. For those lenders still lending to churches, the old lending rules which churches have come to understand and expect are essentially out the window having been replaced by fewer sources of money, a greatly increased level of documentation, much stricter underwriting criteria, and reduced lending amounts.

Today, when a church applies for a loan it needs to be able to demonstrate two important qualifications. First, a history of retained income in excess of what the loan payment amount will be and secondly, sufficient cash to bridge the gap between the loan amount and the project cost. If the church approaches a lender with financial reports that do not demonstrate these two fundamental requirements, they are essentially guaranteed not to get funded.

Lenders have historically required a minimum of 20-30 percent equity investment by the church in the building project. For the purchase of undeveloped land, the lender would typically require an equity investment of 40 percent or more. In the post 2008 economy, both of these percentages are higher, which increases the amount of cash a church needs to bring to the table. The church may find that it needs at least 25-35 percent of equity for construction. This can be a significant impediment to building and increases the burden on the church to become financially prepared to build.

Different lenders will have different criteria on how much equity the church will need to qualify for a loan and how much of the total equity the bank will accept in land equity. Many lenders will often want the church to have some cash in the deal, not just land equity. If a bank's lending criteria is 70 percent loan to value (LTV: the amount of the loan as a percentage of the completed project's appraised value), the church needs cash to cover the difference between the loan amount and the project cost.

One of the best ways to develop cash equity is to execute a capital stewardship campaign (See Chapter 7) well in advance of building. These funds will be designated for the purchase of buying land and/or new construction. This is best started as early as possible, *preferably as much as 2 to 3 years before the church needs the funds.*

Church lenders require more paperwork and detailed financial documentation in order to approve a loan than ever before. Before the lender approves a construction loan, they will need to see proper financial statements that demonstrate how the church will make the monthly payment and show adequate cash to bridge the gap between the loan amount and the total project cost. The income and expense statements will need to show a history of monthly retained income that is 100-120% of the anticipated mortgage payment. Essentially the church will need to show a history of making the mortgage payment to themselves (that is, monthly retained earnings) before the bank will make the loan.

Financially, the majority of churches do not systematically prepare for a building program. Most do not have enough of the building program cost in cash or even a plan in place to raise the cash before building. The vast majority of churches run what may be referred to as a zero sum budget; they typically spend everything they receive. Unfortunately a zero sum budget does not leave room for a mortgage, nor does it help the church accrue cash.

Unless the church has a cash surplus at the end of every month that is at least the amount of the future mortgage payment, the leadership will need to do some financial engineering to equip the church to accommodate this additional expense. There are only three basic ways to financially address this issue.

1) Reduce expenses - look at areas where cutbacks can be made in spending in order to grow the church.

2) Increase giving - usually by increasing attendance and through teaching stewardship principles.

3) Reduce project cost - reducing the project scope and/or implementing design concessions to reduce cost.

In the final analysis, once the church has accurately totaled its income and expenses, made the necessary expense reductions, and worked on increasing giving through teaching and practicing good stewardship, the church will then be able to determine a monthly loan payment it can afford. The following table provides some shortcuts that give a good approximation of borrowing capacity.

To determine the church's estimated borrowing ability with a 20-year commercial loan, take the monthly payment the church believes it can afford and divide it by the factor for the interest rate the church believes it can obtain. The resulting answer will be your approximate borrowing capacity.

Interest Rate:	Divide payment by:
5%	0.006599
6%	0.007164
7%	0.007754
8%	0.008364

The resulting answer will be the approximate amount your church could borrow at that interest rate for 20 years. As this table demonstrates, by working backwards from a maximum monthly payment, an estimated loan can be easily calculated.

The examples in the following chart demonstrate how interest rates will affect the church's borrowing capacity for a given payment amount. In our example we will use a modest $7,000 per month payment to calculate the various loan amounts (rounded to the nearest dollar).

Borrowing Power Estimation:

Interest Rate:	Loan Calculation:
5%	7,000/0.006599 = $1,060,767
6%	7,000/0.007164 = $977,108
7%	7,000/0.007754 = $902,760
8%	7,000/0.008364 = $836,920

As shown in the previous table, for a monthly mortgage payment of $7,000, the church would be able to borrow approximately $836,920 at 8% interest and $1,060,767 at 5%.

Using our simple budget estimator, if we plug a middle value of the $977,108 of borrowing capacity into the loan amount along with the other known financing variables, we end up with a project budget of just over $1.3 million.

Cash on Hand	125,500
+ Cash You Can Raise By End of Construction	200,000
Cash From Sale of Assets	0
+ Financing (Loan or Bonds)	977,108
= Total Estimated Building Budget	$1,302,608

Remember: The maximum loan amount will be based on the <u>lesser</u> of what the church or the bank believes the church can afford.

Your total building budget is what I refer to as your bucket of money. Every cost associated with your building program gets paid out of this bucket. It is important to remember that the church's maximum project budget must cover <u>all</u> the costs associated with the building program, and not just the building. It is easy to overlook or not prepare for all the costs involved in a building program.

These costs include, but are not limited to:

§ Professional consulting fees

§ Architectural and engineering drawings

§ Surveys and environmental reports

§ Permits, fees, and licenses

§ Inspections

§ Land acquisition

§ Land clearing and site work

§ Wetland mitigation

§ Road improvements

§ Stormwater management

§ Building construction

§ Construction interest

§ Fire suppression

§ Utilities and/or septic and well

§ Moving and relocation expense

§ Furniture and fixtures

§ 10 percent contingency buffer

As was pointed out earlier in this book, counting the cost requires an understanding of everything that needs to be counted. *Accurately counting the cost requires the experience to do so correctly and is assisted by an objective viewpoint.* It is in the church's best interest to insure that the right questions are asked and answered in order to insure that the church's needs are met in the most cost effective manner.

Vision is a future destination, usually realized over time in incremental steps. The example I used earlier is that of the Lord delivering the Promised Land to the tribe of Israel. His vision of the land for them was a sure promise delivered as they *needed* it. Like Israel, the church's vision for building may exceed its current financial ability. In fact, I would expect this to be the case in more building programs than not.

What the church builds must be based on what it needs and what it can afford. If the church's vision is bigger than its bucket of money, the proper course of action may often be to build what is needed most right now and then build the rest as the Lord gives the church the increase. In order to properly conceptualize this, it will be helpful to develop a master plan that shows the church's best prediction of the future building phases. This will also help insure that you place the current building in the right place on the site as part of a larger plan.

A conceptual master plan will also help communicate the overall vision to your congregation. *Remember, a picture can often do what a thousand words cannot.* Communicating clearly is absolutely critical to visioning, developing focus, and raising money. A master plan demonstrates how the vision will be worked out over time. Your current financial ability and building budget determines how much of that vision is built in this phase.

The two primary methods of financing church construction are traditional lending and bond offerings. Either of the two financing methods is available in a variety of flavors. With a traditional loan, the church is essentially borrowing all the money from a single source - the bank or lending institution. In a bond offering, it is borrowing money from a large number of investors.

Conventional Financing

A traditional loan is one in which the church goes to a lender (like a bank) and receives a loan that is usually based on two primary factors: the church's current cash flow and the collateral value of its assets (including the future value of the new building facilities).

In a conventional loan, the lender will evaluate a multitude of criteria using multiple underwriting models to determine a maximum loan amount, interest rate, and payment terms that they would possibly offer the church. The criteria they will evaluate will often include, but is not limited to:

§ Total income

§ Net income

§ Number of giving units

§ Giving per giving unit and/or giving per person

§ Attendance trends

§ Historic giving patterns

§ Value of assets

§ Credit history

§ Whether you have run a capital campaign or not

§ Cash on hand

§ How long the church has been in existence

Of all of the criteria the lender will evaluate, the single most important is the church's regular monthly net cash flow, the difference between income and expense.

> Make no mistake, the primary criteria the bank will use to qualify your church for a loan will be based on past documented income and demonstrated ability to make a loan payment.

In the past (pre-2008), the church would look at its discretionary expenses to see where it could cut back in order to make the loan payment and then convince the lender how they could find the money to service the loan. Today, churches have to demonstrate their ability to make a mortgage payment by already showing retained earnings, month in and month out, that are somewhat greater than the proposed mortgage payment.

As a general rule of thumb, the lender will want to see average monthly retained earnings (or earnings transferred into a church account) that are about 110-120% of the proposed mortgage amount. This is commonly referred to as the debt service coverage ratio. A ratio of 1.1:1 would mean the church would need to show retained earnings of 110% of the loan payment amount. A debt coverage ratio of 1.2:1 would mean that for every $1,000 dollars of debt payment, the church would need to show a history of having retained $1,200.

Financial Tip: At least one or two years prior to building it would be good practice to put a line item into the budget for servicing a mortgage payment. Try setting the amount as close as possible to what might reasonably be the future loan payment. This is a great way to accumulate savings in the building fund for the new facilities. Further, when applying for a loan, this amount will demonstrate the church's ability to service debt.

For a conventional loan, the amount of money that can be borrowed will be limited by the church's current income and cash flow. Cash flow is the difference between money coming in and money going out. If, on a monthly basis, the church has $10,000 income with $9,000 in expenses, the net monthly positive cash flow is $1,000. If your church brought in $300,000 and spend $300,000, then your borrowing capacity is very easy to calculate – it's zero!

A lenders' first consideration is to how the church will make the mortgage payment from its <u>current</u> cash flow. This is the primary criteria by which a lender will evaluate the church's financial ability. The second major qualifier is lenders will probably not loan more than a certain percentage of the value of the property (including the completed project). This limit can vary by lender, but post-2008 it is usually in the 65 to 75 percentile range. This is called the *loan to value* or LTV. Lastly, the lender will want to know you have *adequate cash* **reserves** in case something does not go as planned.

Outlined below are a few things that should be watched for in a conventional loan agreement.

§ Origination fees. Typically this amount should not be more than 1 to 1.5 percent and can often be negotiated down to a lesser amount.

§ Personal guarantees. Avoid them unless there is just <u>absolutely</u> no other option.

§ Prepayment penalties. Generally speaking, this is something you should avoid at all cost.

§ Variable interest rates. Be careful here. At the time of this writing, rates seem to have more or less bottomed out. While no one knows the future, common sense tells us that rates have a lot more room to go up than down. As a general rule, if interest rates are not expected to fall in the next few years, variable rates are generally not a wise solution.

§ Balloon or call date. While the loan may be calculated on a 20, 25, or even 30 year amortization, the entire loan may be due at some predetermined date, typically between 3 and 10 years, with a last payment equal to the then unpaid balance. This generally requires the church to re-qualify for a loan in order to refinance the remaining balance on or before the balloon date.

Financial Loan Package

Preparing a high-quality financial package is vitally important when seeking financing. Contrary to what many churches often provide, the financial package is more than just a statement of income and expense. The purpose of the financial package is to answer questions the lenders will have, *before they ask*, and to portray the breadth, depth, and financial ability of the ministry in the best possible terms.

Loan rates and terms are determined and money is loaned based on perceived risk. A properly prepared financial package should demonstrate professionalism and creditability which can help give the lender confidence they are dealing with a knowledgeable, capable, and finance-worthy church. In addition to being a great aid in building confidence and respect for the church in the eyes of the lender, a complete and well-organized financial package can significantly speed up the lending process.

A financial package should be comprehensive in scope, incorporating, among many other things, summaries of a needs and feasibility study, cash flow analysis, attendance information, documentation on the capital campaign, history of the church, balance sheet, and resumes of the church staff.

Financial representations must be accurately detailed and supported by clear documentation. A good financial package will not only help a lender make a quicker decision, but is a tool which may be used by the church in negotiating lower fees, better rates, and better terms. A consultant or loan broker can really help a church shine in this area. Note, however, that for any loan that a broker arranges, the church will typically be charged a brokers fee anywhere from 0.5 to 3 percent of the loan value.

When you are ready to talk to a lender, you will want to check with the bank you do business with of course, but also look for lending institutions that specialize in church lending. Often times you will find smaller local or regional banks much easier to do business with than larger banks.

Bond Offerings

A bond is an interest accruing debt instrument issued by the church for a period of more than one year for the purpose of raising capital by borrowing from investors who purchase the bonds. In a bond offering, the church will borrow money by offering to sell bonds to individuals and institutions who loan the church money by purchasing the bonds as investments. The church will deal with a bond company that specializes in putting together and promoting the bond offering. As the bond company sells the bonds, the money becomes available to the church. The church then repays these bonds over time with interest.

There are two fundamental types of bond offerings: public and private. Most churches are familiar with the more common version, the public offering. A *public bond offering* is one in which the money the church borrows comes from a number of people investing in the church by buying bonds with set interest rates and maturity dates. These bonds are purchased in large part by investors and institutions unaffiliated with the church which invest based on a prospectus prepared as part of the offering. These public bond offerings must fully comply with state and federal regulation, including the SEC, with all the required paperwork and documentation. Public bond offerings have high up-front costs for legal preparation and marketing. *It is not unusual to see the up-front cost of a public bond offering be 6-8% of the bond offering amount. This fee is typically 2 - 3% for underwriting fees and a 4 - 6% brokerage or marketing fee.*

Private bond offerings are those in which members and other people closely affiliated with the church purchase the bonds; the bonds are not offered to the general public or outside investors. Regulation of private offerings is somewhat less severe, and marketing is greatly simplified so the cost of preparing and marketing this offering is less than that of public offerings. The net result is that private offerings, while somewhat less common, are less expensive. *The challenge and potential downside of private offerings is the requirement to sell the whole offering to the congregation and to people they know.*

Private offerings may be a very good choice in a church with members who enjoy an above average income, have other investments they may wish to redirect, or would be likely to use this bond offering as part of a financial portfolio. From a spiritual viewpoint, it may also be good for the people of God to divest themselves of secular investments and redirect those investments into the church and Kingdom work.

Church bonds are normally relatively safe investments that create a competitive return for investors on the investment. The advantage of a bond program to the church is usually found in the potential flexibility in the repayment of the bonds. It is possible to have different bonds with different interest rates that mature at different times. This may permit the church an option to graduate its payments over time with lower payments for the first few years and increased payments later on after the church has had an opportunity to financially grow.

> A private bond with low costs and flexible call dates
> can present the right church a very good financial
> option *if* the members and people they know have the
> resources to cover the bond offering.

As stated above, public offerings are much more time consuming and expensive than either private offerings or traditional loans due to the increased cost of marketing and compliance with state and federal regulations.

Be careful when signing up for in a bond program. Many church bond offerings are underwritten on a "best effort" basis. In a bond offering, **best effort means the bond company will not guarantee that the**

*bonds will be sold, how fast they may sell, or that your loan will
ever be fully funded.* In a best effort offering, the underwriter simply
commits to offer the bonds for sale. Slow or incomplete sales of this
type of bond offering can jeopardize the completion of a building
project. Unless the bond company guarantees 100% of the bond
offering, the church runs the risk of not raising all the money it needs
to build or not raising the money as fast as needed. In a best efforts
offering, construction financing is dependent on the bond company's
ability to sell all the bonds. Therefore the amount of the final
financing and the rate at which the church will receive money is not
guaranteed.

Some church bond offerings, however, are issued on a "firm
underwriting" basis. In a firm underwriting offering, the bond
company makes a commitment to buy all of the bonds it cannot sell in
a predetermined time period. This provides the church with a
guaranteed loan that will be fully funded. However, the additional cost
for this guarantee can be significantly higher due to legal fees and
marketing costs. When dealing with bonds, it is important to
remember that because bond offerings are generally less well
understood and more complicated than loans, the opportunity for the
church to make a poor decision is greatly increased.

As we will see a little later in this chapter, do not select bond financing
because of the belief that a lower monthly interest rate is *always* the
better deal. If talking to a bond company, the two first things that
should be discovered are, the <u>total</u> fees and expenses to the church for
the bond offering, and the total cost of the financing over the life of
the bond offering. In other words, how much will the church end up
paying in expenses, fees, principal and interest when it is all said and
done. Having been involved in the past with a number of bond
offerings, I can tell you they are a *lot* of work.

Important Concept: Many bond companies will finance some or all of the fees which they then recoup (up front) from the bond sales. Most bond companies will recoup their fees and profit from the proceeds of the bond offering <u>before</u> the church receives any funding from the bond offering.

> With the possible exception of a private bond offering, the primary benefit of a bond offering is usually *not* lowering the *total* cost.

For the purposes of discussion, let's consider 8% as the overhead cost for a public bond offering. By comparison, a conventional loan may have an origination or underwriting fee of 0.5 to 1.5% (one percent is fairly typical). This is where we are able to begin comparing apples to apples and see that non-interest expenses for a bond program could be as much as 16 times more than that of a conventional loan.

For simplicity of comparison, the following examples assume the church will finance all of its financing expenses. If the church paid cash to cover the expenses, this would reduce the amount of money available for building. This, in turn, may increase the amount of money that the church would need to borrow in order to replace the cash used for up front expenses.

Important Principle: Whether bond or conventional loan, the fees the church pays as part of the cost of financing must be added to the interest cost and then amortized over the life of the loan to determine the <u>effective interest rate</u>.

Let's take our hypothetical church which needs $500,000 and see what happens as we look at financing with a traditional loan versus a bond offering. For the purpose of this comparison, we will use a rate of 7.25 percent for the traditional loan interest rate and 6.25 percent for the bond offering, a not so insignificant difference of 1 percent.

Note: Bonds are not usually all sold at the same rate of interest or with the same maturity dates. For the purpose of this example, we will assume the average of all the bonds would be 6.25 percent. In actuality, the average interest rate may be higher or lower than our example.

For comparative purposes, assume a church will borrow $505,000 from a traditional lender ($500K plus 1% in origination fees). A pubic bond offering where the bond includes an estimated 8 percent in additional expense will mean a total bond offering of $540,000. (These examples assume that the church is financing the expenses associated with the financing.) Right away we see an important difference: the church needs to borrow an additional $35,000 to get the same net amount of money with which to build!

Example Cost Comparison: Bond vs. Loan

20-Year Amortization

		Total Interest	Total of Payments
Loan	$505,000 @ 7.25%	$ 452,936.00	$ 957,936.00
Bond	$540,000 @ 6. 25%	$ 416,640.45	$ 956,640.45

From the preceding table we see that while the church paid almost $36,296 less in interest through the bond program, the total savings over 20 years was less than $1,300!

Note: The above example assumes the unlikely situation where the interest rate on the conventional loan remains fixed for the 20 year term, a very unlikely scenario. The point, however, that cannot be overstated is the church needs to investigate the total cost of financing when comparing different financing options.

The total cost situation changes significantly when bonds are paid off early. Remember, the total cost of the bond offering is spread over the number of years it takes to pay off the bonds. This total cost must include interest expense *plus* the fees and additional costs associated with the offering. The more quickly a bond is paid off, the worse the financial performance of the bond will be in comparison to a loan because the higher up-front costs are amortized over a much shorter period.

When bonds are prepaid early, all the fees and costs of the bond offering are spread over a shorter term. As a result, the true annualized cost including interest plus all expenses often proves to be significantly higher than what the stated interest rate would lead one to believe.

For example, Church A borrows $500,000 plus $5,000 in fees from a lender and is aggressive about paying off their loan and does so in 7 years. Church B needs the same $500K from a bond offering which totals $540,000 (including all costs) and also pays off the bonds in 7 years.

Assuming the same interest rates and expenses as stated in the prior example, and figuring level payments we are provided the following comparison:

7-Year Payoff Comparison: Bond vs. Loan

	Church "A" $505,000 7.25% Loan	Church "B" $540,000 6.25% Bond
Monthly Payment	$ 7,683.67	$ 7,953.50
Total Interest Paid	$ 140,428.28	$ 128,094.00
Total of Payments	**$ 645,428.28**	**$ 668,094.00**

Church B with a bond offering and a stated interest rate of 1% *less* than church A, paid nearly $23,000 *more* in payments over the 7 years.

Lesson learned: If you plan to pay off your debt quickly, a loan will often outperform a public bond offering in terms of total cost.

When the total cost of the bond offering is amortized, using this example, we discover the bond's <u>effective</u> annualized cost over 7 years was approximately 8.75 percent - much higher than the stated annual interest rate of 6.25 percent.

A point worth noting: In a market where interest rates are expected to fall, the loan may be a better proposition since it may be possible to refinance the loan at a lower rate, comparable to the current bond offering, without having to pay the high costs inherent in many bond programs. Conversely, if interest rates are expected to rise and you can get a 20-year fixed rate bond, this could save a lot of money over the life of the loan.

In a bond vs. loan decision, the deciding factors on which is best will be determined, in large part, by how long the church plans to take in repaying the debt and what interest rates are likely to do over that period.

There are two positive features of a bond program that the church should consider when making a financial decision. First, the interest rate can be locked in for the whole length of the bond offering. Today, many fixed rate loans have a call, or balloon payment, that is typically due in 3, 5, 7, or 10 years. If the church is certain it is going to take 20 years to pay off the loan, then there may be an advantage in locking in for 20 years with a bond – it depends on what happens with interest rates. However, if the church plans to pay off the debt in 7 years or so (which it should), then a loan is likely to be the better financial decision. This is something the church needs to evaluate for itself.

The interest rate on a fixed rate loan is fixed until the balloon date or maturity date of the loan, at which time the church renegotiates a loan based on the prevailing rates at that time. *If the church has been aggressive about retiring debt*, it should then be refinancing only a relatively small amount of debt. If the church has retired the majority of its debt by that time (as it should), even at a higher interest rate on the refinanced portion (which should be paid off very quickly), the total cost of the loan may still be less than a bond over the same period. If loan rates go down, then the church is in an even better financial position in comparison to a bond. If, however, interest rates go up substantially, the bond may be the better option. Much of this decision rests on the long term economic forecast.

The second positive feature is that a bond program offers options to structure the payments in such a way as to allow for escalating payments. This allows the church to start off with a lower initial payment and increase it over time by selling different bonds with different rates and terms.

Lesson Learned: Conventional loans may not be much more expensive in the long run than bonds and can be much less expensive if the church is going to retire the debt early. They are also generally faster and easier to set up. The faster the debt is retired, the more important it is to stay away from deals with high financing costs. The down side of traditional loans is that the interest rate is generally only fixed for 3-7 years which means that if interest rates go up, the church's mortgage payment will also go up. Many bond programs will fix the rate for as long as 20-25 years. However, if the church is aggressive about retiring debt quickly, a significant portion of the advantages of a bond quickly wane.

At the end of the day, the church needs to evaluate *all* the up-front and long term costs of the lending options and make a sound business decision based on both the total cost of financing as well as short-term benefits. This brings us to our next point…

Retiring Debt

It is one thing to get a loan, it is quite another to pay it off. With few exceptions, shame on the church that takes 20 years to retire a 20-year loan! *Most churches should have a workable plan to retire their debt in 7 years or less.* Interest is money the church gives to the world to foster the world's economy. That money should stay in the Kingdom to finance Kingdom work.

Stewardship plays a large role in both planning to build and in getting out of debt in a reasonable amount of time once the church has completed construction. Stewardship in planning involves designing only what the church can reasonably afford and then having a plan in place to pay for it. Stewardship in retiring debt involves executing the plan in a purposeful fashion. As demonstrated in the following chapter, the church can be debt free in seven years through good stewardship.

As stated earlier, the church can borrow up to around 3 to 3.5 times its current income (usually calculated on the last year's financial statement). Assuming an income of $500,000, this would indicate a maximum debt for the church of approximately $1,500,000 (assuming the church as the cash flow to support a payment for this size of loan.) Now hold onto that number, as we will revisit this example in the next chapter which addresses the capital stewardship program.

How Much Does It Cost to Build?

One of the most frequently asked questions is, "What does it cost per square foot to build?" The answer to that question is about as easy to answer (and as accurate) as "How far is up?" There is no real way to answer the question of cost until you clarify several underlying questions. This is a hard question to answer, even for finished projects, and here's why…

In order to determine a meaningful value to use for cost comparison purposes, one must first determine what goes into the definition of cost. One person may say the building cost for a finished project was $75 a square foot, another may say $125, **and they may both be right!**

How can two answers that are so different both be right? Well, as one of our past presidents so glibly demonstrated, the answer depends on how you choose to interpret the question. To determine cost per square foot, it must be known what was factored into the cost calculation. For instance, were design fees, site work, permits, construction interest, utility tap fees, landscaping, signage, furniture and fixtures, or other expenses that were not part of the building per se, yet necessary to the project, calculated into the cost per square foot?

In our example of two people giving diverse yet accurate costs to build, the difference lay in what they factored into the building cost. **Without knowing exactly what is factored into the cost calculation, a cost per square foot estimate is meaningless at best and deceiving at worse.**

Design considerations and location can sometimes make huge differences in cost per square foot. A simple 15,000 square foot single story building in rural South Carolina will cost far less to build than a similar building in metro Washington DC or Orange County CA. Similarly, a simple yet well built building may cost half or less that of a similarly sized cathedral with ornate design and construction. Another design issue that is often overlooked in the cost per square foot calculation is building height. A 10,000 square foot building with a low roof is somewhat less expensive to build than the same building with a

25-30 foot ceiling height, such as you might find in a multi-purpose building. Even simple things such as roof pitch can make a difference. One moderately sized church project was able to save almost $28,000 by changing the roof pitch from 8:12 to 3:12 pitch. In another project an invisible change to the metal building plan saved the church $35,000, a saving achieved for the investment of $1,500 in changes to the architectural plan.

In building a church there are a number of variables that can affect the cost per square foot.

Total Square Footage: There are economies of scale in larger building projects.

Location: The building costs could vary by 30 percent or more for the same church building built outside rural Tennessee as would be built in urban or metropolitan area.

Style and Amenities: Dramatic architectural elements, design features, and amenities can substantially drive up costs without adding to square footage or functionality.

Total Volume: High walls and ceilings and steep pitched roofs add to the cubic footage of the building without changing the amount of square footage of the building.

Special Considerations: Site work, utilities, legal fees, land costs, soil types, topography, landscaping, road access, and number of stories are all factors that can affect the project cost and therefore the cost per square foot.

Site work is a large and extremely variable expense item in a building program. One church may have $50,000 worth of site work expense and another, for a similar sized building and parcel, spend $250,000. For this reason, site work expense is often not included in the building cost. However, this brings up an interesting point. *What the church needs to focus on is total project cost, not building cost.*

Overly focusing on building cost per square foot can be misleading. The building is certainly a large part of the project, but it is far from the whole project. Professionals familiar with church design can reasonably estimate the cost per square foot once the church has done some preliminary needs analysis and developed a conceptual plan, however, the church needs to remember to focus on the *total project* cost, not just the building cost.

There is only one way to really know what the project will cost and that is to complete your architectural and engineering plans to the point where someone can get real bids from the sub-contractors; anything less is a guess.

A Simple Financing Example:

The church owes $200,000 on a piece of land worth $350,000 and has $35,000 cash with which to build its first building. The cost of the building project is $1,000,000 with contingency and the value of the completed project (land and building) is appraised at $1,300,000. If the lending limit was a maximum of 75% LTV, this would place the maximum loan at approximately $975,000. The estimated cost of construction including contingency & paying off the land is $1,200,000. Subtracting the $975,000 of bank financing from the project cost leaves a shortfall of $225,000. Since the church has only $35,000 in cash, it must raise at least another $190,000 to completely fund the project.

Note: In this example, in order to qualify for a $975,000 loan, a church would typically need an annual operational income of at least $300,000 *and* a net monthly cash flow of over $7,000 with which to service the mortgage.

In this example, had the church had less cash or land equity, or if the site work or the construction costs had been higher, the cash requirements to complete the project would have been even greater.

In today's economy, the church typically needs a significant amount of cash prior to starting its building program, especially if buying land and building.

Chapter 7 - Capital Campaigns & Fundraising

A church capital campaign is a carefully choreographed series of events that encourages an ongoing offering for a given period of time above and beyond the current giving of tithes and offerings. A proper capital campaign is biblical in precedent, spiritual in nature, and produces both spiritual and financial fruit.

Many churches have the misconception of what a proper capital campaign is and what it is not. A capital campaign is a process that is designed to help raise money for large capital projects such as construction, renovation, the purchase of expensive items such as vans, organs, stained glass, or playgrounds, or for debt retirement. A properly run capital campaign will effectively raise money from within (and potentially outside) the congregation through giving that is above and beyond the current tithes and offerings. Most importantly, *a capital campaign is at least as much about spiritual growth as it is about raising money.*

What a capital stewardship program is not, is a high-pressure sales pitch used to fleece the sheep of their money. In fact, the focus of the campaign really is not on money per se, it's on communicating a biblical need exists and how God meets that need through the proper stewardship of the time, talents, and treasures He provides through His people.

The Three Pillars of a Capital Stewardship Campaign

A capital campaign should not be based solely on an emotional appeal, but should be a balance of three foundational elements. When God created man He gave him his mind, emotions, and spirit. To maximize its spiritual and financial success, the campaign must successfully address each of these three facets of man in proper proportion. Therefore, the three pillars of a successful capital campaign are intellectual information, emotional excitement, and spiritual truth.

The people who are asked to give to the church's campaign must intellectually understand and agree with the biblical need that is being met as a result of the campaign. Facts and figures on what the church needs to do, why it needs to be done, and how much it will cost must be provided. Additionally the campaign must also clearly communicate how the members are expected to participate. This information should satisfy the rational mind by removing as many intellectual impediments as possible. Successfully addressing the issues of the mind leaves it free to act in concert with the emotions and spirit. Much of the information that is required for this part of the capital campaign will be supplied by the information from a needs and feasibility study.

While the focus of a capital campaign should not be an emotional appeal alone, the emotions do need to be brought into balance with the mind and spirit. Generally speaking, emotions are easily stirred up and swayed, sometimes reversing with little cause. For this reason, emotion must be balanced with the other two elements, as emotion alone will not endure for the long haul of a capital campaign.

A strictly emotional appeal may produce a quick flurry of money and commitments but will soon fade away, just as fireworks quickly flame out after a spectacular start. Those people who are quickly and easily swayed by an emotional appeal to give will, with equal ease and speed, become emotionally attached to other things such as a new car or boat, a new boyfriend or girlfriend, a new house, or other affections. And when the heart settles on another object of affection, it generally takes the wallet with it. For this and other reasons, the campaign must address all three sides of man over a period of several weeks in order to develop a commitment that will stand the test of time.

The final pillar of the stewardship campaign is spiritual. Like a three-legged stool, all three legs are needed for it to work properly. Of the three equal pillars, this one is perhaps a little more equal than the others. Ultimately, a stewardship program is not really about money, it's about helping people make an appropriate faith response to meet a need, as God has equipped them. (See 2 Corinthians 9:8) There are more than 2,000 verses that deal with money and possessions, so there is no lack of material with which to educate and exhort your members.

As the church moves through the various phases of the capital campaign, the people will be called to make a faith response. The Scriptures tell us that, *"Faith comes by hearing and hearing by the Word of God."* Everything needed to teach someone about stewardship comes straight from Scripture. The church's challenge is to both proclaim it and model it in a way that is understood and applicable to the lives of the people in the congregation. The ultimate goal for the campaign is for people to prayerfully consider how the Spirit of God moves them to participate in giving and then to cheerfully give in accordance with His prompting.

A capital campaign is comprised of 5 phases, not all of which are readily visible to the public. The two initial phases of the campaign involve recruiting, selecting, organizing, training a capital campaign committee, and doing the background work to prepare for the public phases of the campaign. The next phase is the public phase, the one that the church body most visibly notices and what most people think of when talking about a capital campaign.

It is during this public phase that the church capital campaign committee provides information, builds excitement, and provides the spiritual equipping to help bring people to an understanding of the need to build and how they will participate in the campaign to meet that need. A campaign is usually capped off with a Commitment Sunday or banquet to collect the pledge commitments and to celebrate what God has done, and will do, in the church. Finally, there is a short administrative phase and then the long-haul of the ongoing collection of pledge contributions, accounting, follow up, and new member assimilation into the campaign.

As described above, a capital campaign is typically broken down into several phases. The time to complete each phase is dependent on the size and organization of the church.

Planning & Recruiting	3 weeks - 6 months
Equipping & Preparation	5 - 10 weeks
Public Phase	5 - 8 weeks
Receiving Commitments	1 to 3 weeks
Collection & Follow-up	Typically 3 years

The phases can go as quickly as the church can move or take as long (within reason) as it must. The 2nd phase will take at least 5 weeks for a very small campaign and 10 or more weeks for medium to larger churches. A longer period of time is usually less stressful and more effective than trying to cram it all into a few weeks. A longer preparation phase also gives the church more time for the critical task of donor development.

Once the church moves into the public phase, events need to stay on a more rigid timeline. This phase of the campaign is a carefully choreographed time that is intended to maximize the effectiveness of your preparation. For most campaigns, recruiting, preparing, and equipping the stewardship committee should start at least 4-6 months or more before the church wishes to be in front of the congregation with the public phase. Doing so will make the whole process much easier, less stressful, and generally improve the overall quality of the campaign.

What You Should Expect

Most churches should expect to experience most or all of the following in a professionally run campaign:

§ Spiritual growth and increased faith.

§ A pledge commitment of 1 to 3 times the current annual income in tithes and offerings.

§ A greater understanding of God's perfect plan of providence and stewardship with a corresponding dependency on His Word.

§ An increase in normal tithes and offerings of 10-15 percent. (This may dwindle over time if stewardship principles are not taught on a regular basis).

§ A greater sense of unity and purposefulness in the congregation.

It must be noted that a primary presumption of a capital campaign is that the church has a good idea of what it wants to build, why it needs to build, and what it can afford. *If the church cannot definitively answer these questions, it is premature to run a capital campaign.* The "what", "why" and "how much" of the building program are critical requirements for the intellectual and spiritual components of your campaign. Trying to run a campaign without these critical components is like trying to run your car with missing spark plugs.

The Financial Benefits

Over the past several decades, thousands of churches have executed professionally facilitated capital campaigns. Historically speaking, churches have typically *raised between 1 and 3 times their current tithe and offering income* over three years through a purposeful and professionally facilitated capital stewardship campaign. This is in contrast to fundraising which provides more modest revenue to the church from the sale of goods or services.

Ignoring for the moment the tremendous *spiritual* benefits that result from a capital stewardship campaign, there are at least six ways a church building program will *financially* benefit from a capital campaign.

1. Some churches may use a capital campaign to begin a savings program in order to pay cash and avoid debt.

2. Some churches, in order to expand the scope of the building project, may opt to augment their borrowing capacity with additional funds from a capital campaign.

3. Some churches, without the necessary cash to begin a building program, may use a capital campaign to help raise the necessary cash to cover up-front expenses and/or necessary cash buffer prior to securing a construction loan.

4. Some churches will choose to use a capital stewardship campaign to pay off the debt as quickly as possible.

5. A capital campaign provides a fund from which a portion of the higher mortgage payments may be paid until the congregation and giving grow to meet the payment.

6. A capital campaign may be required by the lender in order to qualify for a loan.

Let's consider again our example church from the previous chapter which had $500,000 per year income and look at what happens when the entire proceeds from a capital campaign is applied to debt reduction.

In that example, it was determined that conventional lending guidelines would indicate that a maximum safe debt for the example church might be $1,500,000. Given historical precedent from other capital stewardship programs, it would not be unreasonable to expect this church to raise between $500,000 and $1,500,000 over the next three years in a professionally facilitated capital stewardship campaign.

If we took a conservative viewpoint and said the church raised only 1.5 times its current income (which is more typical in the post 2008 economy), at the end of three years the church could retire as much as $750,000 of the $1,500,000 debt by applying 100% of the proceeds from the campaign to reducing principal. During this same time period, the church will have reduced its principal balance by at least another $127,703 through its regular monthly loan payments, leaving an unpaid balance of $571,101 after only 3 years. (*This assumes on time mortgage payments and additional annual payments from the capital campaign applied against the principle of $250,000.*)

As shown by this example, the combination of regular payments plus the proceeds from the capital campaign has enabled the church to retire just over one-half of the debt by the end of the three-year campaign. Of course, if the church raises more money in its campaign, then the remaining debt is reduced correspondingly.

It seems reasonable, therefore, to expect that if the church can retire half of its debt in three years, it should certainly be able to retire the remaining half over the next four years. In fact, if the church were to continue with its regular payments and then run a second campaign with similar results to the first, it would easily pay off the loan balance in 6 years and have some seed money for the next building program already in the bank.

Being optimistic, I believe the church will grow numerically and financially over the period of paying off the debt. This is supported by a study of churches that showed 80 percent experienced growth after completing the building program. Increased attendance should translate into increased offerings which should allow the church to retire its debt even more quickly.

Being practical, I also realize that many churches will elect to augment their building budget with some of the proceeds from the campaign, or use some of the campaign income to help service debt, either of which would leave less of the proceeds for debt reduction. This notwithstanding, the principle is still a valid one.

The church in our example executed a second stewardship campaign that was a non-stop continuation of its first campaign. That campaign paid off the remaining debt and put money back into a building fund account for future renovation or building programs. Hopefully your church will be considering its next expansion plans before the end of seven years, which is certainly a very good reason for becoming debt free as quickly as possible!

Becoming debt free in seven years or less begins with the concepts discussed earlier about knowing what is needed and what can be afforded. The church needs to do this *before* getting too far into a building program, and then put a plan into place to make it happen. **Part of the financial plan for any building program should include a plan to retire the debt in a timely fashion.**

Many churches elect not to hire outside help for a capital campaign. For the vast majority of churches, this decision is often to their financial loss. Conventional wisdom and anecdotal evidence indicated that churches that use a professional campaign consultant/coach raise, on average, twice as much as churches that self-deliver their campaign. *While there are exceptions to every rule, my personal experience confirms that churches inexperienced in capital fundraising which do not use outside consultants typically raise about 50 percent less in their fundraising than those who do get professional assistance.*

In 2010 I had an opportunity to put this to the test. A church that had been in discussions with me about a capital campaign elected to do it themselves. My initial fact-finding indicated the church could likely raise $1,000,000, and the church only needed $900,000 to make the numbers work for their project. About 8 months later the church called me. Their campaign had not performed as they expected, raising just over $470,000, and they wanted to know if I could help them meet their goal.

I had never had the opportunity to do a "do-over" campaign for a church, but was confident we could improve their results. Long story short, we ran a "second wind" campaign and raised the total to just over $800,000. While not quite double, and perhaps not as good as they could have gotten doing it the right way the first time, I believe this fairly represents the difference between well intentioned and well qualified campaign leadership.

As this demonstrates, it is to the church's advantage to hire a capital campaign consultant to assist with the fundraising. Any increase in the cost of the campaign due to hiring a consultant is certainly offset many times by the increased giving that results from this assistance.

When Should the Church Run a Capital Campaign?

With few exceptions, the answer to this question is generally "as soon as possible." In the post-2008 economy, a capital campaign may be required by the lender, or may be required to provide the necessary cash on hand and cash flow to qualify for a loan. The money raised before construction can either be used to reduce the amount of money the church needs to borrow or to increase the scope of the building program. How this money is utilized depends on the church's interpretation of financial stewardship, and of course, the church's unique situation.

Finances are the biggest limiting factor in most building programs. If planning to build in three years or less, now would be the appropriate time to start becoming financially prepared. As it is written in Ecclesiastes 3:1, *"To everything there is a season, a time for every purpose under heaven."* The scriptures also direct us to consider the ant who, *"Prepares her food in the summer and gathers her provision in the harvest."* (Proverbs 6:8)

The bottom line is that the church needs to be financially prepared when the season of building comes upon it. Too many churches struggle, or even fail for a time, because of lack of timely preparation. There are several reasons to execute a stewardship program well in advance of building.

§ A building program and capital campaign are both complicated and time-consuming events, and both deserve undivided attention.

§ By starting sooner rather than later, the church will have more money with which to build.

§ The increased giving to the building fund *may* be factored into the loan calculations, potentially increasing the amount of financing the bank may offer.

§ A demonstrated pattern of giving to a building fund improves how lenders rate the risk in lending to the church. This can potentially improve the loan rate and terms.

§ A capital campaign creates a sense of excitement and unity.

Another consideration for the timing of a campaign has to do with the time of the year. There are times in the year when, in the typical church, a campaign is more effective than others. The church should take care to organize the campaign around holidays, vacation times and other church events that might compete for the time and attention of the staff and/or members.

Retiring Debt Is More Expensive Than Avoiding It!

An important point to note is that a dollar given in advance of the building program is more valuable than a dollar given to reduce debt. For every dollar of debt that the church assumes in a building program, it will cost significantly more than a dollar to retire it. For example, at a 6.5% interest rate, every dollar of debt will cost $1.25 to retire *if* the loan is paid off in 7 years. If the church takes 20 years to retire its debt, every dollar borrowed will end up costing the church $1.79 to retire.

Two important questions that need to be asked of the membership as it prepares for a capital campaign are these: (1) Who gives to the church building fund in a capital campaign, and, (2) Who pays the mortgage every month? The bottom-line answer to both these questions is that the congregation does.

If the congregation has the option of giving a dollar now to avoid debt, or giving as much as $1.79 to pay off a dollar's worth of debt, which would they rather do? It comes down to paying a dollar today or as much as two dollars later.

> Would your members rather contribute $1 now to avoid having to borrow it, or pay $1.79 later to retire $1 worth of debt?

This logic, however, does not apply if the church is electing to use the capital stewardship funds to extend the scope of the building program instead of retiring debt. In this case, the capital campaign merely permits a larger project to be built than would otherwise be possible but does little or nothing with regard to retiring the debt more quickly.

Fundraising

Not to be confused with a capital stewardship campaign, which is a purposeful long-term offering, fundraising is a shorter-term program (or series of programs) in which money is given in exchange for goods or services provided with the profits going to the church. Fundraising events come in a variety of different shapes and sizes from candy bars, bake sales and chicken dinners, to car washes and rent-a-youth.

Fundraisers are a good way to keep financial needs fresh in people's minds. It also gives the church a way to encourage members to approach people outside the church to ask them to help with the building program. Through fundraisers, the congregation and community are given multiple opportunities to contribute financially to the building fund. Don't think, however, that this type of fundraising will replace a capital stewardship program.

The most effective way of raising money for the building program is through the determined, sacrificial, weekly giving by the congregation through a purposeful capital stewardship program. Fundraisers *can* raise money for the building program; however, fundraisers will not be the *primary* source of funding a new church. After all, it takes a lot of candy bars or spaghetti dinners to pay for a church.

Fundraisers are great ways to raise money for various aspects of the building program including new furniture, sound systems, stained glass windows, new audio/visual equipment, or things that the church may need to purchase that may not be in the building budget. And it goes without saying that the church always has the option to apply the proceeds from the fundraiser to the building cost with the goal of either reducing the amount of money the church needs to borrow in a construction loan or retiring debt more quickly.

In summary, a capital campaign is the most effective way of raising money and reducing the amount of money the church needs to borrow, and/or helping pay the loan off as quickly as possible. Fundraising is no substitute for a capital campaign, but is a complementary strategy that, when used in conjunction with a capital stewardship campaign, will enable the church to raise the most money possible for this important work.

Chapter 8 - Construction Methods

While the focus of this book is on pre-construction preparation, there are issues regarding construction delivery methodology that require due consideration during the preparation phase. Once the church has an understanding of what it needs and can afford to build, it will then be time to find an architect and a builder. This chapter should help start the church thinking about which construction delivery method is more appropriate.

Other than the church constructing the building itself (which I strongly discourage), the three primary methods of building are design-bid-build, design-build, and construction management. As a general rule, I discourage churches from trying to build it themselves because, apart from a lack of experience and knowledge, the leadership of the church typically does not have the time to invest. I believe pastors and leaders were raised up to preach, teach, and minister, not to be builders. If a person were called to be a builder, then they would probably be one!

> **CAUTION:** Pastors and leaders must not fall into the trap of becoming ***unduly*** involved in the building process. The primary role of church leadership should be spiritual development, not construction. Don't get sucked into the black hole of day-to-day building oversight at the cost of the spiritual health of the church.

Churches that consider self-delivery generally have little idea how cold and deep the water is when entering into a building program. In a recent seminar I did on preparing to build, I recounted the saying "ignorance is bliss" and made the point that there are a lot of happy churches at the *beginning* of building projects, but very often the bliss quickly fades away to be replaced with harsh reality.

Note: When it comes to self-delivery, I will freely admit there are exceptions to almost every rule; *however, its long odds are that you and your church are not one of them.*

A construction project is broken down into divisions. Prior to November of 2004, there were 16 divisions. Since then it has been expanded into 50 divisions. Just to give you a simple taste, here is a list of the original 16 major divisions that make up construction projects.

Division 01 - General Requirements

Division 02 - Site Construction

Division 03 - Concrete

Division 04 - Masonry

Division 05 - Metals

Division 06 - Wood and Plastics

Division 07 - Thermal and Moisture Protection

Division 08 - Doors and Windows

Division 09 - Finishes

Division 10 - Specialties

Division 11 - Equipment

Division 12 - Furnishings

Division 13 - Special Construction

Division 14 - Conveying Systems

Division 15 - Mechanical

Division 16 - Electrical

A project check list we use for a construction manager managing a church building project has 650 items on the list, and each one has to go right in order to build the church correctly. If by some chance you could name only 100 items from this list (can you??), you would still miss 85% of the points. It's a perfect example of the fact that *what you don't know will hurt you.*

There are several ways for a church to contract for the design and construction of a new facility. Depending on size and scope of the project and the goals of the church, one method may be more appropriate than another. Each of these delivery methods is recognized as being *potentially* appropriate.

Design-Bid-Build

Churches may be the most familiar with the delivery method known as design-bid-build. In the conventional design-bid-build model, the church works with an architect to design the facilities. Once the design is complete to the satisfaction of the architect, church, and local regulatory authorities, the design is sent out for bid. Competing bids are received and the church selects a general contractor to build their church. Quite often a general contractor has an estimator who is estimating for all subcontractors based on their knowledge of the market and the subcontractors with which they normally work. The bid is typically a "fixed not to exceed bid" where the financial risk of construction is transferred away from the church and onto the builder. (Or is it? Read on to find out.)

Because each step is done in sequence, the builder has no input in the design process before the construction drawings are completed. This is an important distinction. Changes made during the design process are normally far more cost effective and less time consuming than those made later. Changes made late in the process are usually reactive in nature and often done to prevent and/or manage a negative situation. (See diagrams in Chapter 1.)

A key point to understand is that design changes will occur during the design and permit approval process regardless of the delivery method. However, the construction contracting method can impact the cost of those changes by dictating when they happen, that is, whether earlier or later in the design process.

Construction costs, as estimated by the architect, are far less accurate than the actual bidding process. In my experience, many architects do not have a real good grasp of actual real-world construction costs (an opinion that is frequently articulated by builders). This often results in a building design that is more expensive to build than the church can afford. If the construction cost is found to be more expensive than the church can afford, then the church must go back to the design phase resulting in additional expense in money and time.

The brutal reality of the design-bid-build process is, in my experience, *at least* 4 out of 5 churches who have completed the design process find the cost to build exceeds their financial ability. It is not unusual to hear the church's plans exceed their financial ability by a factor of 2 or 3 times.

One of the few positive aspects of the design-bid-build arrangement is that the builder and the architect both work for the church (as opposed to design-build). This provides a relationship that promotes independent oversight and accountability between design and construction. As can be seen from the diagram following, there are checks and balances between the designer and construction firm, with the church being the mediator.

While this balance can help with keeping honest people honest, it also provides an occasion to have design and construction issues discussed in a forum where the church is caught between two differing opinions.

This can be confusing to the church if it is not equipped to understand the advantages and disadvantages of the differing positions or solutions presented by the architect and builder.

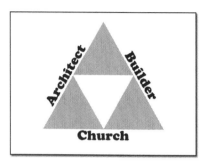

Design-Bid-Build Model

The design-bid-build methodology places a burden on the church by making it responsible for sorting out these differences of opinion between the architect and the builder. These disagreements can cover a range of topics including aesthetics, functional, or structural issues. These differences can also become exercises in finger pointing and blame shifting when something goes wrong. In the design-bid-build model *the church can find itself mediating issues it is not equipped to understand.* This is definitely an area in which an owner's representative, member of the church in the construction trade, owner's agent, or consultant can be a real benefit to the church.

There are two potential advantages to this development method. First, the church gets to (hopefully) select a best of breed vendor for both design and construction. Secondly, in a design-bid-build model, the church, the designer, and the builder are in "dynamic balanced tension" with each other. Ideally, like iron sharpening iron, each is the better for the oversight and input of the other.

In design-bid-build, the church needs to negotiate separate agreements with both the designer and the construction firm. Design-bid-build will often cost the church more than other design methods, especially if the church does not have the experience and know-how to properly manage the bid and contract process. With the design-bid-build method there are more challenges in communication, cost control, defining which vendor is responsible for which issues, arbitration of differences in opinion, and of course, time efficiency.

Another potentially significant problem with design-bid-build is *the designer has no responsibility for the actual cost of the project.* The church may have determined it has a $1M budget which was duly communicated to the architect. However, despite assurances to the contrary, when the church gets the construction bids it may find the bid cost is much higher than the architect's estimate. In this case, unless the church was very wise in its contractual arrangement with the architect, the architect and/or engineer has no liability, and the church's only option is to get the plans redone, usually at substantial additional cost.

Once the project gets started, the builder's primary focus and concern is to have the building completed at or below the bid price. Any cost savings achieved or contingency not used is often retained by the general contractor. This contracting method is normally a "closed book" fixed price contract where the church does not know all of the actual costs associated with its building campaign, only what it is charged by the builder.

Design-Build

Design-build presents a simpler solution for most churches and is one that can potentially provide time and cost savings. Design-build is a development method whereby one firm is responsible for both the design and construction of the project. This method more closely reflects how churches were built through the ages when master builders oversaw all aspects of design and construction.

In a typical design-build model, the church typically hires a builder who in turn, hires an architect, or the architect may already be an employee of the construction company. In design-build, the architect and builder are working together during the design process. This often produces a better result with less cost and time. Design changes are typically made earlier in the process, cost estimates should be known and controlled earlier in the process, and any value engineering that might save money should also be discovered earlier in the process. These all work in the church's favor to save time and money in the project. Many of the time and planning disadvantages of design-bid-build are taken out of the equation.

The problem with design-build is the architect works for the builder, not the church, making the builder the architect's client, not the church. In this arrangement the builder and the architect share a common financial and business interest in the project.

Design/Build Model

Since the church is not the client, the very real possibility exists that design changes may be facilitated to benefit the builder and not the church. There is at least an implied or potential conflict of interest because they have a shared financial goal. Once the project gets started, the primary goal of the team is to deliver the product at or below the "fixed not to exceed price" that was quoted.

This method too is often a closed book fixed price contract where the church does not know all of the cost associated with its building program. The general contractor normally controls the money since one check is provided by the church from which the subcontracts and suppliers are paid. (Sound familiar? It is the same process as design-build-build.)

I have often rendered the opinion that design-build is a much better solution than design-bid-build, which I generally consider the worse construction contracting method for a church. Some advantages for the church in a design-build relationship are:

§ A single party is responsible and may be held accountable for all aspects of design, cost control, timeline, and quality, from design to dedication ceremony.

§ The potential for improved communication between the design and construction teams.

§ Fewer contractual relationships to negotiate – saving time, effort, and cost.

§ A streamlined process and (typically) a shorter timeline to project completion.

§ Increased efficiencies which provide cost savings that should be passed along to the church by the design-build firm.

§ Avoids "finger pointing" between designer and builder.

§ Typically less work for the church.

In summary, the design-build methodology certainly offers some potential benefits in keeping with the goals of the church in saving time, effort, money, and stress, over that of design-bid-build. *The largest potential downside to design-build is that the church has all its eggs in one basket.* Since the architect and builder are on the same team, the church may find itself without the potential benefit of the dynamic tension inherent in the checks and balances that design-bid-build is capable of providing. If the church makes a bad decision in hiring a design-build firm, the church can be in serious trouble.

One of the valid concerns with design-build is the potential for the architect and builder to make decisions in favor of the bottom-line of the design-build firm, without the church's knowledge or consent, to the possible detriment of the church. If the church elects a design-build delivery method, it may be wise to invest in third party oversight (owners representative) to help the church keep good honest partners good and honest, and to help watch out for the other kinds.

Some additional drawbacks common to both design-bid-build and design-build:

§ Owner gives up line item by line item knowledge of cost and cost control which often results in higher overall project costs.

§ Knowledge of cost savings achieved by the GC is unknown and not generally passed through to the church.

§ Owner gives up financial control by placing each construction draw in the hands of the GC, who then must pay the subcontractors, who in turn must pay the suppliers. This multi-step chain must work every time for the church to avoid financial liability.

§ Owner perceives that most, if not all, of the financial burden has been passed to the GC, when in fact a significant amount of risk remains with the church in exclusions or allowances that may not be adequate.

§ Change orders are outside the scope and quoted price of the fixed price agreements.

The last three points above concerning financial risk need to be explained in more detail. When a subcontractor performs work, or when materials are sold to a job, there is a lien placed against the church for the value of those goods or services. When payment is received, a lien release is provided to the church. If the church pays the builder, the builder is to pay the subcontractor, and the subcontractor pays the material supplier. With these payments comes (supposedly) the lien release from each of the subcontractors and vendors. If the builder fails to pay the subcontractor, or if the subcontractor fails to pay the supplier, <u>the church is still liable for the payment even though it paid the builder</u>.

In the post-2008 economy, too many builders and subcontractors are on the edge of insolvency. Any time a builder is in financial duress, the temptation exists to use your money to pay off another bill. Your lender may require the church to bond its builder against just this eventuality (at additional cost, by the way). A bond is essentially an insurance policy and it takes time to work out any claim and receive payment. Meanwhile, your project could slow to a halt, costing additional time and money. Eventually it will all get straighten out, but not without cost to the church.

In a fixed price or not to exceed bid, certain portions of the building costs are *estimated* as "allowances" or possibly excluded. Sound, lighting, and flooring are just some of the common allowances. The allowance for each of these may be woefully inadequate and the church may find that an acceptable quality and quantity of these items may cause the cost to significantly exceed the builder's allowance. The church is responsible for any additional cost above the allowance. In this case, the guaranteed fixed price isn't so fixed after all. Allowances and exclusions vary greatly from builder to builder and project to project. The point is that fixed-priced contracts may not be as fixed as the church perceives.

If you give it fair consideration you will probably agree with these two conclusions. 1) The builder is more experienced at this than you are, and 2) The builder is going to do everything they can to make sure *they* don't lose money. So at the end of the day, you will probably find the builders' contract provides *them* the ability to avoid undue financial risk. That does not mean the risk goes away; that risk needs a home, and if the risk is not with the builder, that only leaves the church!

Once the project is bid, any changes to the building plans requested by the church or required by building code is at additional cost. These are called change orders. And unlike the original project, change orders are not sent out to bid. Once you have a contract with a builder, you pretty much lose your ability to negotiate price or seek bids. Sad to say, there are some builders who will bid a job low knowing in advance there will be many change orders (having reviewed the plans) and will have the chance to significantly increase their profits in no-bid change orders.

In summary, any of the above points can increase the cost of the building project past the "guaranteed" price for either design-build or design-bid-build.

Open Book Construction Management (OBCM)

For the purposes of this discussion regarding Open Book Construction Management, we are referring to the construction methodology of OBCM without a fixed, not to exceed price. In this type of relationship, the builder's fee is fixed based on the cost estimates of the project developed during the design process.

I feel OBCM provides the church the best building solution in that it has the highest degree of transparency and cost control. In this delivery method, the design and construction professionals work directly for the church, yet do so in a team approach. This gives the church the advantage of the architect and builder working together from the beginning of the design process but insures that *each works for, and is responsible to, the church*. Working through the design process with the architect allows the builder to have valuable input into the design and material selection, and can provide the team with *accurate* costs estimates during design. In this method, the real costs are known by the end of design as opposed to design-bid-build where this begins the cost discovery process.

Two of the most frequently asked questions of OBCM is, "How does the church get competitive bids, if the construction manager (builder) is selected before the design of the building," and "How is the church protected without a fixed not to exceed price?"

In an OBCM delivery model, the church selects the CM based on their historical ability to deliver church building projects on time and budget, as well as a spiritual and emotional fit. It is the role of the construction manager to get multiple bids for each line item in the building budget. In this manner, the church knows the best price on a line item by line item basis rather than just the lower overall price out of three builder's bids. *Since it is highly unlikely that any single GC in a design-build or design-bid-build arrangement will have the lowest cost in every category, OBCM can produce a lower cost to build – the true low cost in that particular market.*

In a fixed not to exceed bid, there will be contingency added to the actual costs, just as a GC will build a contingency into a design-build or design-bid-build fixed price agreement. In OBCM, at the beginning of the project, contingency may be 10% of the total project cost. However, as the project progresses, the contingency may be progressively reduced as the project progresses on or under budget. The biggest difference is that due to the transparency of OBCM, the church knows at all times the real cost of the project and whether the contingency fees are being used or will be retained by the church. Some of the other advantages of OBCM are:

§ Builder input is early in the process which can reduce time to build, project cost, and can improve the overall design.

§ There is total transparency with respect to bids, awards, invoicing, and payments.

§ Church retains cost control on a line by line item basis.

§ Church retains financial control by placing the check of each draw in the hands of the subcontractor rather than trusting the builder to properly disburse funds. *The builder never handles the church's money.*

§ Knowledge of cost savings achieved by the CM are discovered in the bidding process.

§ Church knows that all unused contingency is retained by the church.

§ 100% of cost savings are retained by the church, not the builder.

§ Architect and CM are hired independently by the church and each is responsible to and represents the owner.

There are those that will say that the church is at higher risk in OBCM as there is no guaranteed fixed maximum price. As has been pointed out, the guaranteed maximum price offered in deign-bid-build or design-build is not as guaranteed as the church may believe. In almost any case, a catastrophic event that might cause a building program to significantly exceed budget in OBCM is also covered by an exclusion or allowance in guaranteed, not to exceed price contracts.

The biggest perceived issue with OBCM is that the church is not as familiar with it. Being a less familiar method (albeit one that is rapidly becoming more popular), churches are suspicious of it and may go with a contracting method they are more familiar with, even at a higher cost.

Selecting a Builder

As the church investigates architects, builders, or design/build firms, ask for references - lots of them. Ask for both older and more recent references, particularly for church projects of the same size, building type, and budget. There are a couple good reasons why you should not hire a builder just because a pastor's buddy had a good experience them. The first is that the pastor's friend may not have received such a good deal and just does not know it (remember the saying "ignorance is bliss?"). Secondly, things may have changed with the builder since the other church was in their building program. The construction business is very volatile and a couple of bad projects can bring a firm (especially smaller firms) to the point of insolvency.

Knowing that things can change quickly, when checking on builders both past and present performance must be reviewed. What that firm did two years ago is great, but how is it doing today? A few basic things that need to be reviewed and verified when hiring a contractor are:

§ Customer references

§ Vendor references

§ Better Business Bureau

§ Insurance coverage

In checking with the vendors and the Better Business Bureau, make sure that the builder has been in business for some time. When checking vendor references, find out how long the vendor has had a relationship with the builder. If the builder has been around for several years, but many of the vendor references are only a few months or a year old, it may indicate a problem. The builder may have had to find new vendors due to payment problems.

Another question to ask the builder is how long they have been in business and then check their response with the state corporation commission. Be alert to name changes. The builder may have been in business 20 years, but if the owner changes the name of the company every few years, it is a definite red flag because some builders have been known to close a company to avoid legal problems and open a new one under a different name.

And as stated previously, consider whether the architect or builder has experience designing and building churches in your size, style, and budget range. A firm that has dozens of mainline church references for multi-million dollar edifices may possibly not be a good fit for a smaller church that is building a multi-purpose facility.

Chapter 9 - Building Guidelines & Rules of Thumb

The following guidelines have been compiled from a variety of sources, including my own experiences of seeing what really works - and what does not. Use these guidelines as a starting point for planning, but please note that these are only general guidelines and every one of these has exceptions or modifiers based on a church's particular needs and circumstances. These guidelines should not be construed as advice on what to build, but should only be used as starting points of reference in the planning and budgeting process.

General Building Guidelines

- In general, a church should estimate approximately one acre per 125 people on campus at one time. This allows space for the building and adequate parking, green space, setbacks, playground, recreation, and stormwater management. This space requirement may be greatly reduced in a metropolitan area where on-street or public parking is available or where many members utilize public transportation to get to church.

- Plan for one parking space for every 2.25 people on campus at one time. This is probably more than the minimum parking required by the city or county, but will more accurately reflect *real need*. Initially a church can get away with fewer parking spaces; however, it will need to plan to provide adequate parking to meet the needs of the total design capacity of the facilities, even if the church decides to grow into it over time. For example, a design for a 300 seat sanctuary may require, according to building code, 1 parking spot for every 5 seats, which translates to 60 parking spots. If you are like most churches, you probably average between 2 and 2.5 people per car. This would mean that your parking capacity would limit you to 150 persons in a sanctuary meant for 300!

- To get an accurate idea of your church's parking requirements in a future building program, have someone go into the parking lot and count cars over a several week period in conjunction with taking a good attendance of *everyone* on campus, including men, women, children, and babies. Divide the total attendance by the number of cars and average the results over a period of several weeks. As previously stated, the result will probably be somewhere around 2 to 2.5 people per car. Divide this number into the design capacity of the new facility, and this will tell how many parking spaces the church will really eventually need in order to fill the building to capacity.

- Estimate parking to be between 90 and 120 cars per acre depending on local landscaping codes. A church of 250 should anticipate needing to park approximately 110 cars, which will require approximately 1 acre of land in order to park the cars on-site.

- Structured parking (parking decks/garages) is very, very, very expensive to build. While structured parking can dramatically increase parking per acre, consider it only as an absolute last resort because of cost.

- Sanctuary seating requirements will range from 7 to 15 square feet per person depending on layout, seating type, seating pattern, and total size of the sanctuary. Stage and chancel area, which may vary greatly between churches, may be calculated separately from seating area based on specific needs. Generally speaking, a good rule of thumb is 12 square feet per person.

- Using chairs instead of pews will generally allow the seating of more people in the same space, perhaps by as much as 20 percent. Chairs also allow for the reconfiguration of the sanctuary as needed to support various uses (weddings, Sunday morning service, special events, community use, fellowship, and etc.).

- The Vestibule/Lobby/Narthex area should be about two square feet for every seat in the worship center. Normally this will be approximately 15 percent of the total sanctuary space. If the church plans to have multiple services, it should consider increasing this space to facilitate the "shift change".

- Classrooms range in size from 12 square feet per person (for adults) to 35 square feet per person (nursery and toddlers), depending on the age group using the space, whether tables are utilized, and general seating style.

- Meeting rooms average around 20 square feet per person and a choir room is about 15 square feet per person, but could be larger if also used as a robing room.

- Almost no church is built with enough storage, janitorial, or work space.

- A high school size basketball court is 50x84 feet. Adding even a modest amount of space around the edge of the court for out of bounds, plus allowing for restrooms and storage rooms means that a church could be looking at 7,000 square feet of building for a multi-purpose facility that will include a basketball court. Add courtside seating, classrooms or multi-purpose rooms, a stage, and a kitchen and this could easily become a 10,000 square foot building or larger.

- Individual staff offices are usually recommended to be a minimum of 120 square feet. The pastor's office should be a minimum of 150 square feet (with a recommended size of 300 square feet). Cubicles in open workspace areas typically range from approximately 30 to 105 square feet, although they may be as small as 4'x4" (16 square feet).

- In fellowship hall seating, using rectangular tables is more space efficient than round tables. While round tables are more conducive to fellowship, round tables in a fellowship hall will reduce seating capacity by approximately 20 percent. In calculating space needs for the fellowship area, plan on 12 square feet per person for rectangular tables and 15 square feet for round. It is also noteworthy that square tables are generally easier to store as well.

- Don't design your fellowship hall for that one-time or two-time a year need or major event. A fellowship hall will typically be sized to seat about two-thirds of your total maximum sanctuary capacity.

- How often do you see a line for the men's room compared to the ladies room? Plan on *at least* twice the restroom capacity for women than for men.

- Hallways should be no less than 6-7 feet wide. Wider halls (10 feet or more) are important if running multiple services in order to facilitate moving larger volumes of people during peak load times. Wider halls are especially important around the Sunday school rooms, an area that is very frequently congested.

- Handicap ramps should have a slope of no more than 1 inch of drop per linear foot unless handrails are provided.

- Plan to budget approximately 5-10% of the building cost for new fixtures and furnishings and then reduce the budget as you identify furnishings that you may reuse if relocating.

- Generally speaking, ground floor space on grade is somewhat cheaper to build than basement or second floor space. To minimize cost, if there is room, it is generally better to spread out horizontally instead of building vertically.

Issues That Drive Up Construction Costs

There are several things in a building program that the church has little or no control over, such as zoning and building codes. However, there are a great many variables it can control. This section will attempt to highlight a few of the issues that tend to increase the cost of construction. These are issues the church should be aware of in its planning and land search process.

Topography: Hilly, sloped, rocky, or uneven terrain, as well as creeks, springs, wetlands, and other marvels of nature can significantly add to the cost of site work. After the building itself, site work is often the second largest cost in a building program.

City or County Location: A church may find that the cost of building outside the city limits is less expensive due to less demanding building codes, landscaping requirements, and a quicker plan approval process (time is money).

Utilities: Extending a sewer or water line to reach the property can be a very expensive proposition. If the sewer hookup is to a pressurized sewer line, you will have to install a lift station, a potentially significant expense.

Roof Height and Pitch: Raising the height of the roof will often incur increased costs in walls and possibly increased foundational and structural support. High pitch roofs also require more material and have higher labor costs than do lower pitched roofs. Increasing the cubic footage of a building also increases building cost as well as ongoing operating cost of heating and cooling.

Fire Suppression: The requirement for sprinklers can increase the cost of water utilities due to requirements for increased water flow and pressure. The total cost of the fire suppression and annunciator system is several dollars per square foot. If the church is on a well, the local fire codes may require a holding tank for water to run the fire suppression system which will add significant cost. So, as the church evaluates potential building locations, it needs to consider water supply issues.

Soil Issues: Soft or mucky soil must be removed and replaced with good dirt. Rock outcroppings may need to be blasted or removed. Soil issues can have a significant impact on the cost of site work and therefore the total project cost.

Multiple Stories: As a general rule, adding additional stories in either a basement, second, or third floor is usually more expensive than building all on one level. Potential savings from a reduced footprint can often be offset by increased costs in excavation, floor trusses, and stronger footings. Multiple floors will also require the additional cost of adding non-productive space such as multiple stairways and elevators in order to comply with ADA and fire safety codes.

Building Materials: Aesthetic design elements such as brick exterior, laminated beams, cupolas, clock towers, and stained glass windows will have a significant impact on the cost of a building without adding a proportionate amount of functionality or capability.

Time: Time can work against you in two ways. Building costs go up each year between 6 and 10%, so delaying construction can be expected to increase the cost of the project. Consider this; in a bad year, postponing a $1M building project might cost the church an extra $100,000 (over $8,000 per month) for one year's delay in beginning the project.

During construction, poor planning or slow decisions on the part of the church can cause costly delays. These delays create increased project cost due to construction interest being accrued on a <u>daily</u> basis. A modest sized building program may average about $150 or more per day in construction interest. Delays in the early part of construction, when the church has a lower construction draw balance, is much cheaper than later in the project when the church has drawn a significant portion of their construction financing and is paying higher daily interest.

Street Access: If the primary access to the property is from a higher speed road, the project will probably incur additional costs for traffic studies, curb cuts (for divided highways), turn lanes, and acceleration or deceleration lanes.

The above points are just a few of the less obvious but nonetheless important things to consider when a church is evaluating locations and building designs.

Chapter 10 - Special Challenges for Small Churches

Every church faces its own unique combination of problems in building regardless of size or income. Larger churches have the challenge of motivating and trying to develop consensus in larger numbers of people, generally have more complex issues to resolve, they have more programs and ministries for which to provide, and other size-related challenges. Younger or smaller churches generally face another set of unique problems when considering a building program. Most of their building challenges stem from too few workers, a lack of building experience, low income, low cash reserves, and difficulty obtaining financing. Though these issues are far from unique to smaller churches, they do seem more prevalent.

Financing Challenges

Churches with less than three full years of financial history will have nearly a zero chance of getting financed through a loan or bond offering. Three years of financial history is the absolute minimum for most lenders (unless you have a co-signer, such as a creditworthy denominational entity), and some require as many as five years of history. For churches that do not meet this requirement, owner financing is usually the only option open to them. (See Land Purchase Options in Chapter 11 for more information on owner financing).

One of the challenges that many churches will face, especially those that are smaller or younger, is that of having little or no cash in the bank with which to build. Overcoming this limitation will require careful financial planning and stewardship.

The borrowing capacity of a smaller church is limited. Given that most lenders will only allow 3 to 3.5 times the church's current income in total debt, a church with an income of $70,000 may only be able to borrow a total of $210,000 to $245,000 - enough for a nice family home, but not enough build a church for a "family" of 200 people. (Of course this example would assume that the church could afford the $1,800 a month mortgage payment.)

A smaller church will generally need to focus on increasing both attendance and giving before trying to build. In this case, the church may want to consider buying land sooner and building later. For more information on this, see the buying land section later in this chapter as well as Chapter 12.

Regardless of the size of the church, incurring too much building debt (or any kind of debt) places too large a financial burden on the families in the church. The smaller the church, the easier it is to overburden the members and the greater the financial risk if just a few good givers leave the church.

> When the church is too close to the financial edge, even a few families leaving (for any reason) can mean the difference between making a mortgage payment and defaulting on the loan.

Accounting Practices

If the church is planning to borrow money with which to build, it is imperative that the church gets its financial house in order. Proper financial accounting is a problem for many churches, particularly smaller ones. In order to qualify to borrow money, the church must first have good financial record keeping and reporting. From a church construction point of view, the goal of financial reports is to demonstrate the financial ability to service debt. The best way to do so is by providing accurate and properly formatted financial reports that demonstrate both financial ability and good accounting process.

Please note that just because the church keeps every check and every receipt does not qualify that shoebox full of paper as an accounting process. If the church properly records every check and every deposit in the checkbook or ledger (with details on what the expense represents), an accountant can create a compiled report for you as needed. This would be the *minimum* level of accounting that the church needs to maintain. Likewise, keeping the books on an excel spreadsheet, even if reasonably accurate, may be acceptable for reporting to the congregation, but will probably not be acceptable to the lender.

I recommend that the church purchase a software package that will do multiple functions such as fund accounting (non-profits do not account for funds in the same manner as businesses) as well as track campaign pledges and contributions, membership, attendance, and events such as baptisms. A good software program will provide a level of accountability for the money the church receives and spends as well as making it much easier to prepare to borrow money.

While it can certainly spend more, the church can buy software for as little as $200 that will meet the needs of most small to medium sized churches. Not only will this program make the day-to-day administration much easier, it will organize and report the church's finances in a way that will make sense to the bank. There are also some web based services that are available for a relatively low monthly subscription.

Note: The church should seek the counsel of a CPA familiar with non-profit fund accounting to help set up the books on the computer, to help insure that the church's records and reports comply with generally accepted accounting principles, and to periodically review the books to insure that transactions are properly recorded and reported.

While we are talking about accounting, I would like to include this important tip. Put all the money the church receives into the bank, including love offerings, pastor appreciation, benevolence, and any other offering or received income; and ***never ever pay cash out of the plate***. There are two reasons for this. If you will remember from Chapter 6, a church can usually borrow up to about 3-3.5 times its income. This means that for every dollar of *documented* tithes and offerings, the church can borrow approximately $3.50. If over the course of a year the church has $10,000 that does not ever "hit the books", then it has shorted itself $35,000 in borrowing ability. The second reason may be even more compelling. The improper accounting and distribution of funds can put the church in violation of federal and state laws and jeopardize the church's tax-exempt status.

Shortage of Workers

Besides dealing with a shortage of funds, smaller and younger churches also have fewer people available to do the work. In most churches (and not just smaller ones), 80-90 percent of the work is done by 10-20 percent of the people. This means that the effort involved in building falls on fewer shoulders, usually those same saints who are already doing most of the other work of the ministry.

In my opinion, the effort required in a building program can have a disproportionately greater impact on smaller churches than larger. In a larger church, if a few leaders become heavily involved in a project, the effect on the church is less noticeable. In a small church, where there already does not seem to be enough time in the week to do everything, the church leaders need to be on guard that the time and effort put into a building program does not impact the health and growth of the church. This is especially true of bi-vocational pastors who are already juggling a busy schedule. Large church or small, it is quite easy for a pastor to get caught up in a building program and forget his first love and first calling.

Buying Land

Many younger churches meeting in rented space have the dual challenges of both buying land and needing to build. Rarely will these churches have the financial ability to buy land *and* build a building. They may be able to do one or the other, but it would take a lot of financial preparation to do both at the same time. While the church may be able to find a ready-to-use building for sale with owner financing, it may be best to assume it will not and try to buy land as early as possible. If a church has land, it can always be sold (often at a profit) if the decision is made later to buy an existing building.

In order to buy land as early as possible, the younger or smaller church may need to implement a combination of two strategies: initiating a capital campaign and looking for land for sale by owner. The more cash the church has to put down, the more likely an owner-financed deal may be arranged. In this case, the capital campaign is used to help build a cash reserve that will prepare the church to purchase land when it finds it. It is very heart wrenching for the church to be offered a deal on a piece of land and not be able come up with the down payment when it is needed. For more information on purchasing land and owner financing, see the next chapter.

It will be much easier to get a loan when the church owns land with equity, has demonstrated an ability to raise money, has developed some credit history, and has at least 3 years of financial reports, than it will be if all the church has are a vision and some faith. I do not mean to downplay vision and faith in building (quite the opposite), but bankers do not deal in vision and faith – you've gotta show 'em the money.

Lease-Purchase – A Financing Alternative

A financing alternative for a church that is having a difficult time qualifying for a construction loan is a lease-purchase. In a lease-purchase program, a developer builds the building within budget constraints that the church can afford. The owner builds the building (and in some cases buys the land as well) and then leases the entire facility to the church for a period of time until the church can qualify for a loan to purchase the property. Often, the owner will use the lease as collateral to borrow some of the money to build so the lease payment must not exceed a reasonable percentage of the total income of the church, or the lender will probably not consider the lease as a valid asset.

Lease-purchase can be a great program for churches meeting in rented space, especially those that already have land. A lease-purchase program is ideal for churches that have the ability to make a payment but cannot get financing. The builder/owner takes the financial risk on behalf of the church to build the building; if the church defaults, they are replaced by another church which can be offered the same lease-purchase opportunity. This is not a silver bullet solution; the church still needs to be able to afford payment, it just provides an alternative to churches that can afford the payment but cannot get financing.

Preparing for the Future

Regardless of how the church eventually ends up financing its first building, the younger or startup church needs to focus on growing both its congregation and giving, and setting aside a portion each month from the operating budget (as the church is able) towards a future purchase of land or building. As the church grows, it should encourage its regular givers to give toward a dedicated building fund. Make this process a regular point of discussion with the core members of the church and weave it into the church vision and mission.

As the congregation continues to grow, look toward implementing a church-wide plan of giving (a structured capital stewardship program) and do not set the bar too low! While many church leaders worry people will take from the offering to pay into the building fund, experience shows when it is done right people not only give to the building fund but will also give more in regular tithes and offerings. Remember, a professionally orchestrated stewardship program should normally raise (over three years) at average of 1.5 times the church's current annual income from tithes and offerings. This equates to a 50 per cent increase in giving *above and beyond the current tithes and offerings!*

Believe it or not, churches often do themselves a disservice by asking for less than they should. I have seen churches try to run their own building fund programs and ask for $50,000 (often missing even this low goal) when it could have been able to raise $150,000 or more in a properly executed campaign. Before the church decides to run its own capital campaign, it should be aware that a poorly executed or lackluster stewardship campaign can inoculate the congregation against further giving, creating resistance to a follow-up campaign, and making it much harder to execute, even with outside help.

Chapter 11 - Purchasing Land

Oh what a joyous time, buying the land God has prepared for the church! Purchasing land is a momentous and definitive time in a church's life. It is laying claim to a place to do the Lord's work - a central point from which to minister to the church's mission field. A land purchase will be an important part of many building programs, and as such, requires a great deal of prayerful consideration.

Like many other things, land acquisition may end up being a compromise between what is wanted, what is needed, and what can be afforded. If you have turned to this chapter without at least reading chapters 1-5 of this book, you have missed some important discussion on these important topics. Please find time to review them before moving forward with a land search or purchase.

How Much Land?

How much land should be purchased is always the question. I have heard it said that the church should buy as much land as it can afford and I agree, *in principle*. Most churches should not consider less than a minimum of 3 to 5 acres. As you read in Chapter 9, a general rule of thumb is that the church needs 1 acre for every 100-125 people. If the vision includes becoming a church of 500, then it should probably be looking for *at least* 4-5 acres. The exceptions, of course, are those churches in metro and urban locations that will have little or no on-site parking due to availability of public parking and/or public transportation.

If the church's ministry includes outdoor recreational facilities such as baseball, soccer, or large playgrounds, then the land requirements will increase. Between the infield and outfield, an observation area, and a reasonable separation from other buildings, a Little League-sized baseball field can occupy nearly an acre by itself. A regulation soccer field can actually vary considerably in size. Soccer is played on a rectangular field, traditionally called a pitch, which must be between 100 to 130 yards long and 50 to 100 yards wide. This makes the area of just the playing field anywhere from 1 acre to over 2.5 acres, not including an observation area.

How much land that will be *needed* is going to be determined by the size of the church, its programs and ministries, the ancillary uses of the land, and zoning regulations. Earlier I stated that I agreed *in principle* with the advice that a church should buy all the land it could afford. Churches start getting into trouble when they *literally* buy all the land they can afford and then do not have enough money left with which to build. I call this situation "dirt rich and cash poor". Too many churches have ended up a with nice piece of dirt and can do nothing with it except either sell and start over or wait several years until enough debt can be retired so they can then hopefully afford to build.

Chapter 6 discussed the concept of financial ability. The church should start with a total project budget that is based on its financial ability and determine how much should then be allocated to land and how much to construction. This is another area in which a consultant or denominational resource can be of great benefit to the church. An experienced consultant will be able to help the church develop an optimum budget for land and construction. Identifying this balance is typically part of the needs and feasibility process.

Remember: The church building budget is fixed. The more money spent on land and/or site development, the less the church will have with which to build a building. The key is to find the right balance between land cost and building cost.

Where to Build?

Unfortunately there is no single easy answer to this question. The church will, of course, want to find a building location reasonably central (or at least accessible) to its core membership. *Sometimes the land a church can afford is not exactly where it wants to be.* If this happens, the church leadership and body need to spend time seeking the Lord's guidance to determine whether He is leading the church to a different place or if the church is to bide its time and wait on the Lord. It is often easier to jump to the second conclusion, but the church needs to look at their vision and mission, pray about the issues, and never forget that man has his plans, but it is God who orders his steps.

In order to find reasonably priced land, the church may consider positioning itself ahead of growth and let the area grow up around it. The church may also look for land bargains within the city limits. Within the city, there are sometimes good deals in or near urban revitalization areas, before property values begin to rise. It may not be the greatest neighborhood when the church builds, but it is likely to improve. Even if it does not, I believe a good church in a not so desirable neighborhood is far better than no church in a good neighborhood. You may also look in areas zoned residential instead of commercial, as in most cases residential land is going to be less expensive than commercial property.

When looking for land, there are a number of things that the church will want to weigh in the balance. For each land parcel under consideration, it would be helpful to the church to create a "scorecard" of the important evaluation criteria and have each of the members of the land search committee score each parcel. This approach will make it easier to compare properties in a more objective manner.

Visibility: The location should be easily visible from the road.

Accessibility: The location should have easy ingress and egress. Just because the church is visible from the interstate does not mean people will take the time to figure out how to get to the church. Accessing the property from high-speed roads will require additional cost in creating acceleration, de-acceleration, and turn lanes. If it is a divided road it may also require cuts through the median. Property that has access from two or more roads is a real benefit from a traffic management point of view.

Shape: A square shaped property is generally the best for maximizing land use. Try to avoid long narrow property and odd shapes as they reduce the usable land space and make site planning difficult.

Zoning: Land zoning is a huge issue. Make sure the land use and zoning regulations will permit the building of a church on the property, without the need of a hearing or special permits.

Jurisdiction: Building within the city limits may be more appealing, but building outside the city limits usually means the land is cheaper and building regulations less stringent, thereby reducing the church's cost to build.

Long Range Planning: That busy little two-lane road today may become a four-lane connector in the not so distant future. The city, county, and state commonly have 3-year, 5-year, and sometimes 10-year development plans. Get to know the local planning department. They can help in understanding where development is heading and where roads are planned for construction or widening. Getting there ahead of development will greatly reduce the church's land cost.

Topography: Sloped or hilly land is more costly to develop than flat land. Watch out for creeks and ponds as they complicate the building process with large environmental setbacks. Even "dry creeks" where there is only water flow during wet weather can hinder the building process and increase the cost.

Neighborhood: If locating in a commercial area, check to see who your neighbors will be. If the land is vacant, it would be a good idea to see who owns and see if they are the kind of potential neighbors the church would want to have. If in a residential area, it would be a good idea to meet the neighbors, particularly if the church has to apply for a special use permit or zoning exception. The last thing the church needs is to meet the neighbors for the first time in opposition at a zoning hearing.

Noise: Go out to the site at several different times during the week, even on a Sunday morning either before or after church service, and see what the noise level is like. Make sure the land is not under an approach to an airport and there is not an unusual amount of heavy equipment or tractor-trailers rumbling up and down the street when the church would be trying to have worship service. This is especially important if the property is not very deep and building away from the road is difficult. Also make sure the property is not too close to anything like a gun club or quarry (both have happened) as, oddly enough, people may find it harder to concentrate on a sermon when they hear gunfire or explosions.

Before purchasing any property, have the successful completion of the following tests included in the contingencies clauses of the contract. As part of the contract to purchase, the church should have a negotiated amount of time to do due diligence and get these tests performed:

- Soil Test. Watch out for rock and bad soil.

- Level I Environmental Survey (including endangered species and wetlands).

- Perc Test. A percolation test is only needed if the building will be on a septic system.

In addition to the above tests, look into the availability and cost of hooking up utilities. It will be necessary to not only check into the availability of utilities but also the cost to bring service *to the building site*. It is not enough to ask if utilities are available; get an estimate of the cost to get it to the building.

> If the church has properly analyzed its needs and financial abilities and knows the general area in which it is called to build, it then becomes merely a process of matching needs to opportunity.

Searching for Land

Once again, there is not only one right way to do this. Land search begins with understanding what the church needs and what the church can afford. This provides the church with a description of the land the church should be looking for and what the church can pay for it. I cannot begin to express how much time and effort this will save in eliminating pointless investigations. If it is determined the church needs at least 5 acres of land and can only spend $150,000, then there is no sense looking at 4 acres for $200,000. Before looking for land, let's put a few myths to rest.

Myth #1: The church needs to wait and not buy land until it is ready to build.

I believe in most cases just the opposite is true, especially for smaller churches that are meeting in rented spaces. For many churches, the financial burden of buying land and building is too great to overcome at the same time. *As stated earlier, many churches can afford to buy land or build but have a hard time doing both at the same time.* It is doubtful that land will never get any cheaper, so a church should try to buy land as early as possible and pay it off as quickly as it can. This will not only reduce the overall cost of the building project, but it will provide needed equity for when the church seeks the financing for construction. It also enables the church to break an overwhelming financial burden into two manageable transactions instead of one impossibly large one.

Take a tip from the big boys... Many of the mainline denominations will buy land outside growing areas several years before the town grows out that far. When the population arrives, the church can build a building on land that is debt free, for which they paid a fraction of the current land cost.

Myth #2: All land is expensive.

Even in areas where land is priced by the square foot (and there are 43,560 square feet in 1 acre), there are opportunities to be had. Developers are sometimes required to set aside land in planned developments for churches, schools, and other community related facilities. It is also possible that someone who has made a nice profit selling other land might consider donating some to your church for the tax write-off. Churches get land donated to them all the time, but no one will give the church land if they don't know it is looking. See the next two sections in this chapter for ideas on how to search for land.

If the church wants to be downtown, land will generally be much more expensive. If the church is willing to move outside the city limits, the price of land will drop sharply in most cases. Moving from a commercially zoned area to one zoned residential can also reduce the cost of land. You will also want to check local zoning codes for which zonings are most compatible with church development. If possible, try to avoid property that will require a change of zoning, special exception, or special use permit, as this can add time and cost to the building process. In considering land, you certainly should give preference to property that is already properly zoned.

Myth #3: A church needs a realtor.

If the church is buying land listed by an agent and *if* the listing agent is unwilling to reduce the commissions (to the church's financial benefit) when the church does not bring a buying agent to the table, then by all means get an agent to represent the church, as it will cost nothing extra.

However, a church does not *need* a realtor to find property that is listed for sale. Information on property listed through a realtor is available through any number of web sites, the most notable of which is www.realtor.com. For MLS listed properties, this provides your church members 24/7 access to most of the same information realtors have available to them. If the church finds a property of interest, the church can view the property and then, if interested, contact the broker handling the listing for more information.

Do not sign a dual agent agreement with the listing agent just because they ask. Tell them the church reserves the right to get a buyer's agent involved <u>unless</u> the realtor would be willing to reduce the commission to be both the listing and selling agent. It may be advantageous to point out that their reduction of commissions may be deductible as a charitable contribution, if done properly.

> If the church is only looking at property listed for sale or that has a for sale sign out front, it is probably missing the best deals on land!

Besides looking for property that is listed for sale through a realtor, there are two other ways to look for land: networking and the Internet.

Finding Land Through Social Networking

As stated earlier, no one is going to give the church land if they do not know the church is looking for it. Networking through the people the church knows, *and the people they know,* can be an effective means of finding land for the church.

There was a popular pastime several years ago called six degrees of separation. It was based on the mathematical theory that anyone on earth can be connected to any other person on the planet through a chain of no more than five acquaintances. No doubt you are wondering how this amazing piece of trivia applies to hunting for land, so allow me to explain. It would seem to stand to reason that if by networking through five friends of friends a connection could be made to someone like Bill Gates or George Bush, then a church should be able to connect to someone in its community with some land for sale!

Let's say you are the pastor of a church with a congregation of 75 adults, and the church needs to buy land. Let's go on to say that you and each of your adult members are on an acquaintance basis with another 40 people outside of the church who live in your area. If there were no overlap in "who knows who," this would directly connect your church to 3,000 people!

To be conservative, let's say there is a 50 percent overlap in who knows whom. Even with that much overlap there are still 1,500 people to contact about land. *If the ministry and the congregation clearly communicate the fact that the church is looking for land to these 1,500 people and encourage them to talk to people they know, it will not take long to get the word into the right ears.* If only half of those 1,500 people talked to only 5 people each, the church's need for land will reach over 3,700 people!

The better a church is at communicating the need, perhaps backing it up with a small pamphlet or handout, the better the results. If a church can take this grassroots approach and make it effective to three or four levels of friends of friends, a church of 75 adults could reach 10,000 people with its need! If you church has 275 adults, think of how many people you could potentially reach, especially in this era of social networking. As the church is about to roll this program out, seek the blessings of the Lord and ask Him to open some ears and prepare a heart to meet the need.

Albert Einstein said, *"In theory, theory and practice are the same. In practice, they are not."* So we know that in reality it won't work as good as our theoretical model. Many of the people in the church may only ask a handful of people, and the numbers go down with every step removed from the church. However, if the church makes it a matter of prayer and consistent reminders to its congregation to talk to the 40 or so people they know, the church should expect to see results. Encourage church members, four, five, or even ten times over a period of a few months to mention it to their network of family, friends, and co-workers, and eventually the need will worm its way to the right ears. Obviously the larger the church and the more motivated the members, the more people can be reached in a shorter time. This encouragement, bolstered by prayer and repetitive communication, can be quite effective in mobilizing your congregation in communicating the need.

Finding Land Via Real Estate Web Sites

The other network to use is the Internet. We already discussed how one could go online and see MLS listed property for sale. There are also several "For Sale by Owner" web sites where one can look for private listings. However, there is yet another powerful option, especially when it is discovered that many times the land sold to churches was not listed for sale when the church bought it!

Many counties and cities have automated their property tax system and make property information available online through a web browser. Most of them have the option of providing a map-based search through what is typically called a GIS (Geographical Information System). Through the county or city GIS system, one can get an aerial view of the area with the ability to see roads and property lines along with owner information – all from your computer.

A GIS system is like a shopping catalog for land! As the building committee chair of my church, I was able to research and compile information on hundreds of properties right from my desk. For each property, I compiled owner contact information, flood plain determination, topographical maps, aerial views, tax value, and in some cases, sales history. I was able to create a binder full of possible church sites without getting out of my chair! The exact information that is available will differ from county to county, but there is a lot of information just waiting to be discovered.

From the computer's aerial viewpoint, streets and roads can be followed and you have the ability to zoom in on land in the areas in which a church would like to build. The size of the land parcel and owner contact information can be determined. Using the owner name and address, an online phone number lookup can be done for published numbers using any number of telephone number lookup sites, such as the one at www.whitepages.com. Other types of information that may be available, depending on the GIS system, are: zoning, sales history, flood plain determination, property photos, topographical maps, soil types, utilities, owner information, renter or owner occupied, tax value, and street view or aerial photographs.

While searching for property, remember that the church will generally have better results buying property that is either undeveloped or that has an older rental house on it than it will by trying to buy the owner's primary residence. Once a list of potential properties and associated contact information has been compiled, it is as easy as picking up the phone and saying…

"Hello, Mr. Smith? This is Pastor Hopeful at Grace Community Church in Anywhere, USA. Our church is looking to find some land on which to build our new sanctuary and I was calling to ask if you would be interested in an offer on the X acres of land you own on Such and Such Road."

Now there are only three likely answers to this question: yes, no, and gee, I hadn't really thought about it. If you get anything but an outright no, see about trying to set a meeting to get to know each other. This will be a chance to build a relationship with the landowner, talk about the great things the church does, and to ask them to work with the church on the land. It also presents a wonderful opportunity to share the gospel!

Note: For landowners whose address of record is a post office box number, a certified letter stating something similar to the above example should get some attention.

One of the advantages of buying land that is not listed for sale is that the owner has not fixated on a sale price or mentally started to spend the money in anticipation of a sale. As such, it might be easier to negotiate a deal in this circumstance than one in which the sale price is more firmly entrenched in the seller's mind. Another advantage is there is no need for realtors, which reduces the expense to the seller, hopefully reducing the cost to the church.

Land Purchase Options

Land deals for property on which to build the church can end up being quite complex, or they may be dirt simple (pun intended). The simplest deal is when the church can pay cash for a piece of land. Actually, that's not quite accurate, the simplest deal is when someone walks into the church office with a deed and donates some property. After that, things start getting a little more complex.

When the church finances vacant land, the lender will probably require the church to have *at least* 40 percent cash or other equity in the property as opposed to the 25% or more minimum usually required for construction projects. If the land appraises for $200,000, the bank is probably going to lend a maximum of $140,000 (and in the post 2008 economy you may be fortunate to get them to finance vacant land at all). For a traditional lender, the church will need to show at least three years of financial reports and demonstrate the necessary cash flow in order to service the loan.

Owner financing of land is a desirable option, especially if the church is younger and/or will have difficulty producing the 40 percent equity or down payment most lenders require for the financing of vacant land. You can use owner financing to sweeten the deal on the purchase of land in the following way.

Let's say Mr. Jones wants to sell a piece of land for $100,000. The church has $10,000 to put down and asks him to finance $90,000 at 7 percent interest. Mr. Jones knows if the church defaults on the payments, he keeps the church's $10,000 down payment plus any other payments the church made, *and* he gets the land back. If the church does make its payments, he will get significantly more than the $100,000 asking price, because he also receives the interest income. If the church took 5 years to pay off the land, the seller would be receiving approximately $18,000 of interest income (depending on the interest rate) on the loan. Effectively Mr. Jones will receive $118,000 for a piece of land he wanted to sell for $100,000.

Owner financing is a generally low-risk opportunity that offers a higher return for the seller. Owner financing can work well if the seller does not owe a large amount of money on the land and does not need a cash infusion from the sale of this property for other purposes, like buying another property.

Note: Owner financing may not work with a seller who owes a significant amount of money on the land the church is hoping to buy unless the church's down payment deposit is greater than the money owed. However, in the right situation, owner financing can be a great financing solution and bargaining tool.

Another option is to offer to buy the land in multiple parcels over time with each parcel having its own contract for sale. Let's say the 10 acres of land the church requires has been found, but it is more than the church has determined it can afford. In most cases, the church will not need all 10 acres today. The church should consider offering to buy 5 acres today and put the remainder under contract for sale with a closing date in the future (perhaps 3-5 years out or more). In this scenario, the church would make a significant good faith deposit on the second 5 acres (say 10 to 15 percent) and perhaps even agree to a premium price (based on today's prices) on the second 5-acre tract. This allows the church to get the land they need today while deferring half the cost of the land until the church has had a chance to grow. The church's growth should provide at a future date both the <u>need</u> and the <u>ability</u> to buy the land.

There are a number of variations on the above scenario, including carving the land into the smallest possible parcels and crafting an offer which includes buying the land in multiple parcels over time. This also provides an option for land donations from the seller (sort of like buy 3 acres and get 1 free) that may provide them a tax benefit. Under the proper conditions, and with some experienced help, it is possible to reduce the total cost of a land purchase by a sizable portion while offering tax advantages to the seller through a combination of purchase and donation. Additional tax savings may allow the seller to realize a net profit equal to or greater than they would have received if the church had written a check for the full asking price of the land.

Owner financing, especially those deals that include some combination of sale and charitable donation of property, have several financial advantages for the seller. The charitable donation of land can help offset the seller's capital gains tax and/or the tax liability from other income they may have. The tax advantages are different in each deal, but it may help the seller to pay less tax when they are able to spread income out over several years in multiple smaller sales rather than to take a lump sum payment.

When the circumstances are right, creative land purchase deals may permit the seller to net as much or more than was anticipated, while the church pays less for the land. The only entity that does not profit from this type of arrangement is the IRS. Properly done, these deals are perfectly proper and legal according to the IRS' own rules! Creative land purchase contracts can save the church considerable money, but it takes some experience and know-how to properly put the deal together and communicate it to the seller. In these cases, the seller's CPA can be a significant help in crafting the deal.

Another potential option is for a small number of the core members of the church to form a partnership and buy the land for the church. This group would use their personal credit to purchase the land, and then write a contract for sale to the church, contingent upon it being able to obtain financing. The church would pay down the debt on behalf of the members until such time as it could obtain its own financing to buy the land from the members for the amount of the remaining loan balance. This is a course of action that should be a last resort and should involve the fewest number of absolutely solid, dedicated members as possible. It should also be properly set up and reviewed by an attorney to minimize the risk both to the members and the church.

Religious Land Use (RLUIPA)

In several areas of the country, churches are experiencing increased resistance about where they are allowed to build. In some cities, zoning regulations have nearly prevented churches from building in their traditional residential settings, often forcing them to areas which are potentially less effective for their ministry.

In 2000, the church received a valuable legal tool with which to counter this growing trend, the Religious Land Use and Institutionalized Person Act of 2000, commonly referred to as RLUIPA. A number of states also offer a state version of this protection, perhaps under a title such as the Religious Freedom Restoration Act. The state RFRA Act offers similar and complimentary protections to RLUIPA.

Under RLUIPA, the church is provided three important protections. The first major protection is found in Section 2(a)(1) of the Act, which states:

> *"No government shall impose or implement a land use regulation in a manner that imposes a substantial burden on the religious exercise of a person, including religious assembly or institution ...unless the government demonstrates that imposition is due to a compelling governmental interest and is the least restrictive means of furthering that interest."*

What this means to the church is that the government cannot, as a general rule, deny a church the use of any land regardless of its zoning, as doing so would place a substantial burden on the church by limiting its religious expression. Unless the government can show that denial was both necessary, due to some compelling government interest, *and* the least restrictive means of achieving that interest, then the officiating body could be found in violation of federal, and possibly, state law.

The second protection offered to the church is found in Section (7)(b), which specifically states:

"The use, building, or conversion of real property for the purpose of religious exercise shall be considered to be religious exercise of the person or entity that uses or intends to use the property for that purpose."

In plain English, this means that buying property and building a church on it is considered a protected exercise; it is a part of free religious expression that is protected under the First Amendment of the Constitution.

Thirdly, the church is protected by the equal terms clause in Section 2(b)(1) where it states:

"No government shall impose or implement a land use regulation in a manner that treats a religious assembly on less than equal term with a non-religious assembly or institution."

From a land use point of view, your church cannot be treated any differently than other places of assembly such as a school, social club, conference center, or theater. If other places of assembly are permitted uses in a given zoning classification, then a church cannot be denied the use of the land solely under zoning laws. Failure to do so would make the case that the church is not being treated on equal terms with other places of assembly. As an example, a church in Florida was denied a special exception in an agricultural zoning that otherwise permitted schools. Under RLUIPA, this was a clear violation of equal terms where a secular place of assembly was permitted, but not a religious assembly, and the decision was reversed. Case law has a large number of supporting decisions in favor of the church.

Some municipalities are making it a requirement that churches have a minimum of five acres of land in order to build. While having this much land might be seen as a good thing, it is unfair to impose this as a condition to build. On the face of it, it would appear to be unlawful under RLUIPA to arbitrarily impose such a burden on a church, especially if these restrictions did not apply to similar places of assembly in the same zoning classification. If the church has burdens and conditions placed on it that are not placed on other, similar uses, then there is very likely a case to be made under RLUIPA.

If you have any questions or problems regarding land use and zoning, I suggest that you seek legal counsel from organizations such as The Liberty Counsel, The American Center for Law and Justice, The Becket Fund for Religious Liberty, or others that have had success defending the church's rights under RLUIPA.

Chapter 12 - Ponderings & Observations

It is my intent, as this book begins to draw to a close, to share some random thoughts and opinions on things related to building churches. No attempt is going to be made to categorize them in any way; it will be a somewhat free association. Some ideas that I considered worthy of reiteration may be familiar from other places in the book.

I hope you find more than a few nuggets of wisdom in the following and perhaps a chuckle or two. Speaking of which, I had briefly considered an alternative title for this chapter, but Proverbs and Lamentations was already taken.

For your convenience, here are 3 sure-fire ways that are guaranteed to increase the cost of a building program:

1. Poor planning
2. Poor contracting
3. Change orders

It always amazes me how otherwise really smart people seem to become less smart in the aggregate of a church committee. If people made decisions in their lives and businesses like some churches do in committee, we'd still be driving horse and buggies to church. To be effective, keep committees as small as possible.

No executive decision-making meeting should take more than 60-90 minutes. Use an agenda. Make sure people have access to the information they need to review <u>before</u> the meeting, and set an expectation with everyone to be prepared to make a decision. Executive meetings should generally be for clearing up questions, voting, and handing out assignments to the subcommittees.

A capital campaign is less about money than it is about understanding a need exists, equipping the saints with the knowledge of how God provides for needs to be met, and then calling people to make the appropriate faith response. If the members understand and embrace these precepts, the money will take care of itself.

Change can be difficult! There is a natural resistance to change, but sometimes we (the church) struggle *a little too much* with change, making it harder than it needs to be. After all, things have changed a lot in the last 2,000 plus years and they will continue to do so until the return of Christ. Some of the most effective words that hinder a church from moving forward are *"we've never done it that way before."*

Speaking of change, here is a joke I once heard about change in the church. "How many deacons does it take to change a light bulb?" Answer: "Change?? Who said anything about *change?*"

One way to estimate the cost of furnishings is to take the floor plan of your new facility and perform a room-by-room inventory of what you will need to buy for that room. The easiest way to do this is in a spreadsheet with columns for room, item description, quantity, item cost, and total cost (formula of quantity times item cost). Once you have your list, open a church furniture and supplies catalog, assign reasonable prices for each item, and let the spreadsheet total the results, and voilà, you have your furnishing budget!

Lenders are in the business of selling you money. Most often, when you first talk to a lender (well, at least in the past) things sound quite positive. However you should know that this is somewhat similar to walking onto a car lot and talking to a salesman except the lender is there to sell you money instead of a car. However, no lender can really tell you if they can make your church a loan without good financial statements and a review of all the paperwork by the loan underwriters. _Never make any construction commitments until your church has a loan commitment letter in-hand._ The church should always pursue multiple sources of funding to find the best deal for the church.

Something always goes wrong in a building program; it's simply too complicated for it not to happen. Every building program will cost more than you think it should and take longer than you think it should. Anticipate it - plan for it - deal with it.

Churches, on average, seem to be able to afford to build facilities for about 2 to 3 times their current attendance. Your actual mileage may vary.

Make sure you know your priorities. At some time in the planning process you may have to make the decision between bricking the building's exterior and providing additional seating or classrooms.

The executive building committee should not be too large. The optimum size for an executive committee is generally five to seven people. Seven people are generally enough people to spread the work around without making the committee unwieldy. These people can oversee sub-committees where the real work is done and meet as necessary to make decisions.

The executive committee charts the course, hands out work, and makes decisions while the majority of the work is done in subcommittees chaired by members of the executive committee.

Generally speaking, the efficiency and effectiveness of a committee is inversely proportional to the number of people on the committee; double the size and cut the effectiveness in half. So, before you add too many people to the committee, think about how it will probably reduce its effectiveness.

Excessive church voting can really slow down building programs. Your building committee should be empowered to make decisions to whatever level is appropriate. Empower them and then leave them alone to do their jobs without a lot of voting. If the committee feels the need for a vote of confidence, they'll ask. Sometimes church voting gets a bit out of hand, as in the following real-life example.

After moving to a new area, my family and I were visiting churches. At one church of a couple hundred attendees, we heard an announcement for a church vote on whether or not to buy 12 children's chairs for the education department! Can you imagine how this sort of process would hinder a building program?

Churches have split over the color of carpet and whether or not to have stained glass or pews. Having an objective process to determine needs, and then framing potential solutions within the context of the church's vision, mission, need, and financial ability will often peaceably avoid or resolve most conflicts.

A great deal of conflict can be avoided by not letting large numbers of people vote over small details.

If building were easy, everyone would be doing it!

A good contingency clause to put into any contract to purchase land or a building is one stating the contract is subject to approval by a vote of the congregation. It's a great catchall clause that allows the church to get out of a purchase agreement without losing its deposit should something unforeseen happen.

Beware of too many meetings without concrete results. Some good folks are happier to talk about doing stuff than doing it.

Answers are easy. Knowing what questions to ask and what to do with the answers is the hard thing. Like a snake in the grass, it's often the question that you do not ask and answer that will come back to bite you later in the building program.

City or county minimum requirements for parking are usually less than what you will *really need* if you are going to fill up your new building. If you build according to code minimums on parking, have a plan on where you can expand parking when your building starts to fill up. Plan for one parking space for every 2.25 people that will be on the church property at one time. *A half-full building with a full parking lot is usually a waste of building and money.*

If you are planning on multiple services, make sure your parking, foyer and halls are larger than normal to allow additional room for traffic flow during the shift change.

Albert Einstein stated, "*In theory, theory and practice are the same. In practice, they are not.*" Here's a real life example. Going to two services will double your capacity in theory; however, in reality it seems that many churches seem to top out at an increase of about 60%.

Building programs that seem to go around in circles and end up nowhere will inevitably be found to suffer from one or more of these four conditions: lack of real need, lack of good process, lack of effective leadership, or lack of faith. *The first and last are between you and God. A good consultant can help with the other two!*

If you are thinking of letting a contractor who is a member of your church build your new facilities, you should proceed with great caution; often as not this does not end well. If you are considering this, you really should try to talk yourself out of it. If that fails, get someone else to try to talk you out of it.

True Story: A church in NH that had the idea of letting two contractors in their church bid on the project. (Some of you know probably already know where this is heading.) The one who lost the bid got mad, picked up his toys, and left the church. The winning contractor ended up wishing he hadn't and resigned about halfway through the project. For every time using an in-house builder has worked well for a church, there are probably as many times it went the other way. Do you want to flip the coin?? As a member of the building committee, a contractor can be a tremendously valuable resource without being the one who actually has to build the building.

It will probably never be cheaper to build than it is today. I haven't noticed land, materials, or labor getting cheaper, have you?

An outside consultant can be a great lightning rod for comments or ideas that are perhaps unpopular or controversial with some of the members. This can be a great help in maintaining peace and unity in the body of Christ and protecting the church leaders.

If you are saving up for a church construction project, make sure that costs are not rising faster than savings.

True Story: I was contacted by a church that could afford a $700,000 project. The trouble was that they wanted to build a building that was going to cost $1.2M. Rather than build what they could afford, they decided to raise the $500,000 shortfall through a capital campaign. Three years later they had the $500,000 in hand, but with the increase in material and labor costs over time, the project estimate had grown to well over $1.7M. *After three years of saving, they were nearly $100,000 further away from their goal than when they started!*

One of my favorite quotes regarding lowest cost. *"There is nothing in the world that some man cannot make a little worse and sell a little cheaper, and he who considers price only is that man's lawful prey."* - John Ruskin

Rx: Here is a prescription for the health of your building program.
The cheapest price is not always the lowest cost.
Say it out loud
Repeat every day, as needed, to prevent painful results.

When the construction crews are on the church building site, form a ministry team to take them snacks and drinks in the afternoon (except Friday, which is traditionally payday when they often leave early). It will give you a chance to show your appreciation, demonstrate the love of Christ, and share the gospel. You'll probably get a little extra effort and a better building out of it too!

Pastors should not be any more involved in the building program than they feel they must be. God called pastors to teach and preach, not be builders. The pastor needs to look after the spiritual side of building the house, not the bricks and sticks.

Equip your building committee; get some help from someone that is experienced such as a consultant or denominational resource. The people in your church are too busy to reinvent the wheel, so why spend time trying to correctly figure it all out for the first time when someone can help?

Buildings are tools for ministry. Tools aren't always pretty, but they do need to be effective. Too often churches build edifices that are as much or more a monument to the architect, pastor, or building committee than a tool for ministry. God does not care so much how pretty your church building is; he is much more interested in what you do with it. I am not advocating ugly - just a balance in priorities.

Many builders consider churches to be difficult to deal with for two reasons. The first reason is churches typically have a difficult time making decisions, especially in a timely manner. Time is money to contractors. But don't forget that time is money to you also. When the church is paying interest on a construction loan, every day of delay costs more money.

> **Note:** (Warning, dripping sarcasm ahead!) When the church has to have a meeting to elect a committee to research some options to make a recommendation to the deacons to present at an elders meeting so they can call a church vote, it tends to slow down the process a wee bit.

Elect an executive committee and empower them to make decisions within a defined scope of authority. *The church body will squabble less over the decisions the committee makes than it will trying to make the same decisions in a business meeting.*

Secondly, and to its shame, churches often have a reputation for not paying their bills in a timely fashion. Contractors live by cash flow, so pay your bills promptly and remember the ninth commandment when you tell them the check is in the mail.

You can have your church built cheap, fast, or good – you get to <u>pick any two</u>. Construction has three primary variables: cost, time, and quality. You can control any two of these factors but the third will be dictated by the other two. You can have it fast and good, but it won't be cheap. If you want it cheap and fast, it won't be good.

The building permit process can take anywhere from two days to over a year. If you are in the county and have minimal regulations, it can be as little as a few days or weeks. In some high-density metropolitan areas, it can take as much as a year or more. Typically we expect it to take around 90 days.

―――――――――――――

You are not going to please all the people when you build, so don't get upset when not everyone is happy. Do what you know to be the right thing and resist giving in to an overly vocal minority.

―――――――――――――

You know how to tell a goat from a sheep? A goat is always going "but, but, but!" One upset goat makes more noise than 100 contented sheep.

―――――――――――――

Sometimes when certain people leave the church it can be a good thing. Said another way, there are those special people who advance the cause of peace and unity by their absence!

―――――――――――――

Why didn't they teach you this in seminary? Pastors are taught how to exegete the Word, they learn church planting and church growth strategies, and are taught pastoral care; but no one teaches them what to do when they are successful and need to build. (If you are interested, contact the author about seminars and speaking engagements).

Don't buy a metal building out of the back of a magazine! *Anyone who tells you that you can build a 10,000 square foot church for $86,000 is lying or deceived.* One of the largest and best-known steel building companies lost a class action lawsuit for fraud and deceptive sales practices. *(See*

State of Colorado v. General Steel Domestic Sales, LLC, dba General Steel & Capital Steel Industries, LLC, dba Capital Steel)

Regardless of the company, ads for factory closeouts and overstocks are most often gimmicks to separate the church from its money. With the increasing price of steel, metal is almost an investment, so it's doubtful that anyone is truly overstocked or doing factory closeouts.

I have witnessed and heard far too many horror stories: churches with piles of steel rusting on the ground because they can't afford to erect and complete the building, huge advance deposits paid to "protect a special price" where the church cannot get their money back when they realize the truth, building projects half complete because no one understood the complete cost to finish the project, and so many more. The science fiction writer Robert Heinlein coined the word TANSTAFL, an abbreviation for, "There Ain't No Such Thing As Free Lunch." If it sounds too good to be true, it probably is.

"Men often oppose a thing merely because they have had no agency in planning it, or because it may have been planned by those whom they dislike." - Alexander Hamilton (1755 - 1804)

Almost every building proposal put forth in the church will have its naysayers. However, if the majority of solid, sold-out, fruit producing saints in your church are prayerfully behind the building program, go for it. Let those in opposition decide on whether to join you, get out of the way, or find a new church to hinder.

It is my opinion that more churches should consider Christian day care and private Christian schools. I believe there are both spiritual and financial justifications for this.

From a spiritual perspective, I believe we need to provide a Christian alternative to public education where our children, who are being placed under the yoke of anti-Christian rhetoric, man-centered theology, and physically dangerous circumstances. A daycare or private school is also a wonderful way to reach into the community and meet a need while also sharing the Gospel. It can also help financially support a church and provide a resource for home school groups. I believe that most churches could justify offering these services on the spiritual merit alone, however there is also a financial benefit.

Many churches invest significant money in Christian education spaces that, for the most part, sit empty 6 days a week. The two largest expenses that a day care or private school have are rent (or mortgage) and payroll. Since the church has already built the space, it can essentially subsidize one of these two major expenses of the school since it is already paying for the education space.

Having owned and operated an early childhood education center, I can tell you with confidence that a Christian day care or early education facility can significantly add to the finances of the church. Properly run and with the rent subsidized by the church, I see no reason at all why a properly run, modest sized center of 60-70 full time children should not be able to add thousands of dollars to the church income every year and do so at a competitive rate.

Churches that are financially supporting their day care or school are just not doing something right (unless you are offering low tuition as a ministry). Most often, the church can turn a center around by getting the right director to run the program. The director is the key person in the success or failure in almost every daycare or pre-school and is the one most likely to be responsible for the center being profitable, or not. A daycare or school must be run as a business if it is going to pay for itself. A Christian education center can help retire the debt on the building, it can provide a safe haven for children, and it can win souls for the Lord that you might not otherwise reach.

If you build more than one story, there are things that can make the same amount of net useable square footage more expensive than if you built on one level. For example, basements require excavation and waterproofing of walls that can more than offset the savings in additional foundation and roofing. Additional stories require stronger footers and foundation. Any multi-story church will require stairwells (usually two to comply with fire code) that cost as much per square foot as the rest building but do nothing to add to functionality. Handicap access required by Federal ADA requirements may mean that you have to add an elevator or chair lifts *in addition* to the stairs. The addition of stairs and elevators mean that you have to have more total square feet of space to achieve the same net usable space if it were all on one level.

Fire code compliance becomes more expensive from a suppression and annunciation point of view. Some states limit the types of use for education space that is not on ground level. For instance, in NC you cannot have childcare or education space for infants or young children in basements or 2nd stories; these rooms must open directly to the outside on grade. In general, try to go out before you go up.

In most churches, it seems that 90 percent of the work gets done by 10 percent of the people, or if you are fortunate it may be 80/20. Unfortunately it is usually this same 10 or 20 percent who will also be involved in your church building program. It's in the best interest of the church (and these helpful few) to do everything it can to equip these good saints for the work of building.

If you take a vote on building or other important issues and the vote is not overwhelmingly in favor of the resolution, <u>do not move forward</u>. A house divided will not stand. Moving forward on a controversial issue with a church vote of 55 percent may be the first step towards involuntarily planting a new church.

On the other hand, don't hold out expecting 100% support either. God is not a God of confusion. Generally speaking, if less than 80-85 percent of the congregation is in agreement on an issue, it's probably a good time to back up and build unity before proceeding.

Show me in your bible any place where the sheep told the shepherd where to pasture. Since it doesn't, what then does that say about church governance? It seems that congregational votes are a burden that many churches have brought upon themselves. The members are asked to vote on issues of importance, however, the very people who are making the decision are not the ones who sat in the meetings, prayerfully considered the options, did the research, or participated in the discussions. The funny part is, I have attended and served in Baptist churches almost my entire Christian life. God does have a sense of humor!

What this means to the congregationally led church is that before you take anything to a vote, there should be a time of information sharing, discussion, and a venue for questions and answers. A great forum for this is the town hall meeting format. Invite your folks into the church for a time of fellowship and information sharing well in advance of a business meeting and vote. It will develop consensus and support, and it will help ensure you have a more informed vote.

A building program is not a replacement for evangelism. If attendance is in decline, building is seldom the solution. Unless the building is in very poor condition and falling down around you, and that is why people stopped coming, chances are it is not the building that is the problem!

Becoming prepared to build involves spiritual preparedness, vision, financial preparation, and an understanding of future need.

Seek wise counsel. If getting outside counsel was a good idea for Moses and for Solomon, it's probably a good idea for you as well!

Appendix A - Readiness Assessment

This assessment will help evaluate your church's readiness to build and suggest remedial actions as appropriate.

Do you have adequate land on which to build? A good rule of thumb is 1 acre per every 100-125 planned attendees on campus at one time. This assumes you will park everyone on your site, maintain a reasonable amount of green space, and have room for stormwater management. If you are unsure about the land's ability to support the vision, a needs and feasibility study would be indicated.

Do you have an average adult attendance of at least 100? If you do not have at least this many people in the church, you may have too few families to risk a building program. A general rule of thumb for even a very modest church building program would be what I refer to as the "100 cubed" rule. Before you get serious about building, you should be at least 100 adults, with at least $100,000 annual income, and $100,000 or more cash on hand to apply to a building program. I would consider this to be the minimum criteria in order to consider entering into a building program.

Do you have an objective, fact based understanding of what the church can afford to build? See Chapter 6 for the components that make up a preliminary church building budget. If you are not already putting the equivalent of at least the amount of your future mortgage payment into savings each month, you need to become financially prepared to build. You need to reengineer your finances and probably need to run a capital campaign. Financial analysis is an important part of needs and feasibility assessment.

Do you have, or will you have, at least 10-20% of the anticipated project cost in cash prior to construction? If not, you will certainly need to run a capital campaign in order to become more financially prepared to build. A capital campaign is an important part of every church's financial strategy to build and manage debt.

Have you already started a capital campaign? If your church has not already embarked on a professionally assisted campaign, you should do so as soon as possible. If you are not sure where to start, googling "church capital campaign" should get you started. Remember, trying to save money by doing it yourself almost always results in significantly reduced results. If you save ten or twenty thousand by doing it yourself and reduce your results by $200,000 or more, how much did you think you really saved? A professional consultant will help all but the most experienced churches greatly improve their financial results and help make a deeper spiritual impact on the church members.

Do you have complete and accurate financial reports that conform to generally accepted accounting principles? If not, you will want to get your books in order before you show them to a lender. You only get one chance at a first impression, and when money is difficult to get you need to do everything right. Showing up with your books in Quickbooks® or on a spreadsheet won't get you very far and conveys a lack of professionalism. Since you will have to get your financials right before you get a loan, you are better off walking in the door with them correct the first time.

Do you have an objective and fact based understanding of the projected space needs for each ministry? Don't assume the architect will know to ask or know how to determine this for you. It is the responsibility of the church to know what it needs and why. This information and the church's financial ability will largely define the building program. If you do not have an objective space plan that also meets your budget, your church should complete a needs and feasibility study.

How Ready Are You?

One could argue that if you did not answer yes to <u>all</u> seven of the above questions, there are steps you must take before you are prepared to build. However, there are extenuating circumstances that would allow for some latitude, depending on which of the readiness criteria the church did not meet. For example, if you had insufficient land but are sitting on a boat load of cash – well, enough cash can fix a number of other issues. If you are short on land and cash but selling your current location, that fact may offset the other two issues. *The bottom line is that well over 80% of the churches who contact me wanting to build are not prepared to do so*, and pursuing a building program before you are ready can eat up a lot of valuable and precious time, energy, focus, and money.

Appendix B - Insights on Achieving a Positive Church Construction Experience

An Analysis of Select Findings from the Facility Impact Research Study (FIRSt Report)

In 2005, the Rainer Group was commissioned by The Cornerstone Knowledge Network to study the impact of building programs on churches. From the resulting study of 321 churches came several interesting facts that must be taken into consideration for any church that is contemplating a building program.

While an exhausting analysis of the study is beyond the scope of this article, there are three points that warrant special consideration *and application* by the church.

The first point is that many church leaders expressed concern after their building program, feeling that their builder had encouraged or guided them to build facilities that were too small.

Quoting from the FIRSt study, *"...the single greatest regret expressed was that the expenditures were too low and the projects too small."*

Later in the report this thought was repeated, *"We consistently heard that church leaders felt that church builders encouraged them to build too small. There is a sense that church builders are erring on the side of caution while church leaders would like to take greater steps of faith."* While one must be careful not to infer too much from too few comments, these quotes seem to indicate an underlying problem of understanding who is responsible for which issues in a building program. While the input of the builder is important, it would appear from these statements that many churches might have relied on the builder for financial expertise outside of their core competency.

Seeking counsel from a builder on construction issues is wise, but how many builders (or architects) have the financial expertise and in-depth understanding of the church's financial situation to direct a church on how much building they can afford? First of all, it's just not part of their core competency, and secondly, the financial ability and maximum project budget should have been resolved before serious discussions regarding design and project scope were begun with the architect and/or builder. In all honesty, I doubt the builder was the one that financially limited the church; it was most likely the lender. The builder is the last guy in the chain and often gets blamed for things that rightly should be attributed to the architect or lender – or perhaps even the church!

To fault builders for erring on the side of caution when providing advice outside of their area of core expertise (if that were even the case), is grossly unfair. Would the church instead prefer to find itself in financial hot water to the detriment or even demise of the ministry because the builder thought they should build a bigger building? It would seem infinitely better for the church to build additional facilities at a later date, than to risk going "belly-up" sooner. To be honest, in church building programs it is much more common that the builders and architects have to be "reigned in" to stay within the budget than to recommend too small of space. After all, the more they design or build, the more money they make.

The church may realize in hindsight that they might have been able to afford a bigger building program because of giving or growth that could not have been guaranteed before the building program began. Hindsight is 20-20, and it is reasonable to assume that in most cases the church, lender, and builder probably pushed the financial envelope as far as they could based on the financial information available at the time.

The flip side of that approach is the danger of churches "betting the ministry" on future numerical growth in order to finance the building. According to the same FIRSt study, 80 percent of the surveyed churches experienced growth from building, meaning that 1 out of 5 did not. Churches that count on future growth to pay for their buildings may lose that bet – and the church.

What a church constructs must be based on ministry needs and done within the context of what it can afford. *The responsibility for knowing what the church can afford and how it will pay for it is the responsibility of the church, not the builder.* The building budget and prevailing construction costs determine the size of the building, and with careful design and the proper construction methodology the church can minimize construction costs.

A conservative budget formula that implements good stewardship principles is fairly straightforward: it is the money you have on hand, plus the money you can borrow, plus the money the church can raise from the sale of assets such as land. Others, perhaps less conservative, would add to this amount the money the church could raise during and after the building program through a capital campaign. This, however, may be arguable from a stewardship point of view in that the money raised through a capital stewardship campaign might be better applied to becoming debt free rather than increasing the size and financial liability of a building program. Since there is no one-size-fits-all solution, this needs to be carefully thought through early in the planning process. Bringing needs, desires, and budget into balance is a key goal of wise preparation which is highlighted as the third point in this article.

Secondly, the church's level of satisfaction was much higher with multi-purpose buildings or multi-building solutions and lowest with dedicated fellowship halls.

Quoting again from the FIRSt study, *"The lowest level of satisfaction tended to be the result of building a fellowship hall that did not have function beyond fellowship gatherings and meals. The highest level of satisfaction surprisingly took place in multi-building projects in a total church relocation."*

This concept was presented again later in the report, *"Multi-purpose buildings bring the greatest satisfaction to church clients after the fact. Before the fact, many churches may lean toward single-use facilities."*

From a recent historical perspective, single use facilities have been the approach of most churches. Single use facilities are "the way we've always done it" when it comes to most church building programs. Parenthetically speaking, "that's the way we've always done it" are seven deadly words in today's dynamic church environment. Multi-use buildings are being driven by two factors: changes in how churches "do church", and rising building costs.

Multi-purpose space is coming to the forefront as the solution of choice as churches adapt to changing styles of worship and new ministry approaches while trying to get the most building for the money spent.

This is not to say that some churches should not build just a fellowship hall or education building to bring the total church campus into balance. The dissatisfaction of many churches in building may often be due to a lack of understanding of the true building requirements (both long and short term) and the possible solutions that may be implemented to meet those needs.

A simple fellowship hall that seats 150 people might be 3,000 square feet with a building cost of between $250,000 and $350,000 (or more), depending on location and stylistic issues. Some people in the church may have misgivings about the value proposition of spending $300,000 for a building they will use on an infrequent basis. However, if a fellowship hall can be shown to help achieve the overall mission and goals of the church, and the congregation understands and accepts the value proposition, then the church can be assured of a higher degree of satisfaction with its project.

In the final analysis, this issue, like the preceding one, comes down to understanding what must be built, why it must be built, what it will cost, and how it will be paid for - all before the church starts to build. This is the fundamental purpose and goal of a feasibility study. Regardless of whether the church calls it a feasibility study, a needs analysis, or some other name, it is a critical step in *any* church building program which leads up to this final point.

The third point is that feasibility studies tend to make for better building programs and happier outcomes.

Quoting from the FIRSt study, "*We did find a strong correlation in overall satisfaction with the building project if a feasibility study was conducted. The disappointment, however, is that only one-third of the churches conducted a feasibility study.*"

When a consultant says there is a strong correlation, the implication is that of cause and effect. In this case, the operative phrase is, "*if a feasibility study was conducted.*" This then squarely identifies a causal relationship. They *were* satisfied <u>*because*</u> they conducted a feasibility study. According to the study, 33 percent of the churches conducted feasibility studies. This correlates very closely to the 35 percent that considered the building process as "excellent" and the 40 percent that indicated the building program created no conflict in the church.

What did the minority do different than the majority of churches that reported conflict and dissatisfaction? The evidence seems to indicate that a feasibility study helped decrease conflict while increasing the level of satisfaction with the building program.

A significant challenge with churches conducting feasibility studies is that most churches are not equipped to perform them in an effective and objective manner. Despite their best intentions, church members typically lack the two very important qualifications of experience and objectivity. With isolated exceptions, most committees do not have the across the board experience in needs analysis, financial analysis, church design, or construction to be effective in performing a feasibility study.

While some members may have some needed skills, as a whole the church is lacking the skills and experience to come to an accurate and objective analysis. Additionally, one person with some experience and/or force of personality can unduly influence the process, especially when there is little or no other experience in the church.

As an active member in the church, objectivity is often hard to obtain and maintain when you are part of the church building committee. Said another way, seeing the big picture is hard when you are *in* the picture. It is difficult to set aside our personal preferences and needs in order to be objective about the needs of the church when those needs do not coincide with our own. Moreover, churches, and particularly churches that have been in operation for a long time, have cultures and ways of doing things that can make it difficult to think outside the box. Unless motivated by a significant outside influence, churches tend to continue to think and do things the way they always have. Planning is an investment that will pay large dividends, including savings in cost and time. One of my favorite sayings is, "Plan well in order to build well."

In summary, a church considering building should invest in a formal feasibility study to: help maximize the church's satisfaction with the building program, insure they get the most building they need (and can afford), and to get the best building to meet the needs of the ministry, the members and the community they serve. A feasibility study provides a plan for execution, brings unity to the church, and becomes the foundation for the design and construction process.

Ben Franklin said, *"An investment in knowledge always pays the best interest."* In the final analysis, it would seem almost certain the investment in proper planning to explore feasibility and needs would be more than offset by the hard dollar savings the church experiences. Added to this saving is the additional non-monetary value of increasing satisfaction, maintaining unity, and reducing stress and effort on the part of the church leadership.

As it says in Proverbs 24:3-6, *"Through wisdom a house is built, and by understanding it is established; by knowledge the rooms are filled with all precious and pleasant riches. A wise man is strong, yes, a man of knowledge increases strength; for by wise counsel you will wage your own war, and in a multitude of counselors there is safety."*

These verses teach us that the wise will seek counsel from many people. It may be prudent to insure some of those counselors are from outside the church in order to help provide an objective and experienced viewpoint.

Appendix C - Giving in the Church: An Analysis of Average Giving per Person

Do you ever wonder how your church compares to other churches in the giving department? Many churches "feel" like their members give sacrificially but have little real objective data on which to make an evaluation or comparison. It does not help that much of the information available on giving is usually measured in the mystical terminology of a "giving unit" or the marginally irrelevant "membership".

Regretfully, the definition of a giving unit seems to be somewhat vague and prone to interpretation. For example: Is a nuclear family with two working and tithing adults one giving unit or two? How about two roommates who each earn an income and tithes? Is this one giving unit or two? Most of us would probably agree the second case is two giving units, but what about the first? The only difference is the first are (hopefully) married. If a couple write separate checks they might well be considered two giving units, but if they combine their giving into one, does doing so arbitrarily reduce the church's giving units by one?

Cash offerings in the plate provide another challenge as there is no way to know if the cash came from one family, five families, or ninety different people. An offering envelope system will help reduce some of the variables but not eliminate them. When discussing giving in terms of giving units, comparisons or calculations based on a vague or poorly defined terminology will always be suspect at best and meaningless at the worse.

Evaluating giving by membership, as many national studies do, has very limited value. Many churches are horrible at purging membership roles. Members who do not regularly attend church will rarely provide any significant financial support to the church, so evaluating giving against membership is pretty much a waste of time.

As a church construction consultant, I have worked with a large number of churches over the years that were looking to build or relocate. One of the many factors I help churches analyze is financial ability. Even though many lenders will often apply a formulary based on giving per giving unit as one of their criteria, I prefer to deal in a simpler unit of measure when doing initial evaluations. Drawing upon my years of being a church treasurer, I went back to a calculation I used to monitor giving patterns. This calculation is based on a simple and effective formula - giving per person.

When initially working with churches that need to build, I always ask two very simple questions.

1. What are the church's average total attendance counting men, women, and children of all ages?

2. What is the church's total income in tithes and offerings last year (or last 12 months)?

Once these two numbers are ascertained with reasonable accuracy, it is a simple process to divide the total income by the total average attendance to determine the average giving per person per year. Over the years, I became aware of what seemed to be a recurring pattern in the relationship between income and attendance. It appeared that for a significant percentage of churches, one could take the average attendance and by adding three zeros arrive at a close approximation of the annual income.

If my theory proved to be correct, this would indicate the average giving was approximately $1,000 per year for every man, woman, and child in attendance. Eventually I decided to put my impressions to the test. Over the years I had accumulated hard data from many churches, including giving and attendance information, into a database. I exported the information into a spreadsheet and did the simple math. I was pleased to discover that mathematical analysis confirmed my anecdotal estimate.

Note: I did my original calculations on giving in 2005 and determined that the average giving per person was $1,038 per person. A couple years later, I heard a speaker at a Baptist Convention state their study showed giving of $20 per week per person – which totals $1,040 per person per year. This independent study gave me a high degree of confidence in the results of both studies. In 2011, I did a similar study using data from 660 churches from which I had acquired information in discussions about building. The 2011 numbers indicate giving per person of $1,234 per person per year, or about $24 per person per week. This change represented an increase in giving per person of 8.4% over the 6 year period since the previous study. However, once we adjust for inflation, the news is not so good. In the 6-year time period that giving went up 8.4%, the inflation rate went up 11%. It would appear there was a net decrease in giving per person of 2.6%, once one adjusts for inflation.

Interestingly, there appeared to be no significant correlation between the size of the church and giving per person. In fact, in the 2011 study, the top 10% churches in giving per person ranged in attendance from 25 to 1,000.

It is important to remember that averages are just that, an average. There are churches with giving per person well above the average and those that are well below. The churches in the analysis were primarily protestant, evangelical churches in the eastern half of the United

States. The analysis included downtown, mainline churches, small independent churches in the cotton or tobacco fields of the Deep South, and everything in-between. Economically, the churches ranged from dual income families in major metropolitan areas to financially challenged areas where unemployment or social security was the primary source of income for a significant percentage of the church.

What does this mean for your church? It is impossible to say how this information can be applied in an "across the board" fashion to all churches. One area in which this information can help is in trying to predict the church's future financial ability in order to service construction debt as the church grows. If your average giving per person is $1,100 per year and you can add 200 people in an expansion program, what might that do in helping you retire your construction debt? Please note this does not in any way advocate betting on future income; that is, taking on too much debt in the hope you will be able to afford it at a later date! While a recent study of over 300 churches, which had recently completed building programs, indicated that 80 percent of churches grew after completing construction, it also means that 1 church in 5 did not grow!

Each church must take the information presented here, perform their own giving analysis, and apply it to their situation. If you feel your church is above average in financial ability, but giving is less than average, you may want to consider how to better communicate the blessings of good stewardship. If you feel you are right on the mark with respect to the averages, you may decide you don't want to be an "average" church and look to bless the Lord (and your congregation) by striving for excellence in giving.

How blessed is the man who finds wisdom and the man who gains understanding.

Proverbs 3:13

My hope and prayer is that you have found a measure of wisdom and understanding in the pages of this book. May the Lord bless you as you do all that which is according to His will.

About the Author

Steve Anderson has served his church in a variety of roles, including: administrator, treasurer, building committee chairperson, capital campaign chairperson, teacher, and small group leader. He also currently volunteers as a church building consultant for the NC Baptist Convention. Since 1999, he has ministered to churches as a church building consultant assisting churches prepare for building and capital stewardship programs.

Steve is the founder of AMI Church Consulting which was merged into Church Development Services, LLC in 2010. As a principal of Church Development Services, Steve serves as the director of the church consulting division. He is also a seminar speaker, webinar host, author of the Abundant Giving capital campaign program, and has been a contributing editor for various church industry magazines.

Contact Mr. Anderson:
By email: steve@PreparingToBuild.com
Twitter: @YourChurchGuy